Education at Risk

Garth Allen

CASSELL

Cassell
Wellington House   PO Box 605
125 Strand   Herndon
London WC2R 0BB   VA 20172

First published 1997

British Library Cataloguing-in-Publication Data
A catalogue record for this book is available from the British Library.

ISBN   0-304-33834-6 (hardback)
       0-304-33835-4 (paperback)

Typeset by Action Typesetting Ltd, Gloucester
Printed and bound in Great Britain by Redwood Books, Trowbridge, Wiltshire

15.94

EDUCATION AT RISK

_____

Also available from Cassell:

G. Allen and I. Martin: *Education and Community: The Politics of Practice*
M. Fullan: *The New Meaning of Educational Change*
G. Haydon: *Teaching About Values: A Practical Approach*
I. Lawrence (ed): *Education Tomorrow*
S. Ranson: *Towards the Learning Society*
E. Sotto: *When Teaching Becomes Learning*

Contents

Foreword

Risk assessment is where a commitment meets a caution, where potentials are weighed against the destructive power of problems. From its beginnings in insurance to its calculations in management it has largely come to be a means of measuring the private costs of private wealth. Now, for education, Garth Allen has turned risk assessment upside down: there is the public value of political and professional decisions for the public institution of education. The risk in a policy failure is more than a waste of money, it leads to the wasting away of people's good will and then their capacity for goodness.

That, says Garth Allen, is a challenge worth confronting. He does not moan and wring his hands. This is not a thunderous protest that the government has got it wrong. Essentially, this book is about how an economist unravels the value to democracy of some of the knottiest difficulties of the day. There is a lot to choose from in a lifetime of socially responsible research. Garth Allen has always had one foot in research and the other in the management of learning. He has also chosen research projects in which he could be stretched to the limit. The three sections on teaching, children and higher education are cross cut with his abiding concerns for values, for special needs and for the social responsibilities of Higher Education.

It would be tempting to box up this book as if it were only the highly individual achievements of a successful polymath: as if it were a travelogue to be read on cold winter's evenings. But it is much more than that. Garth Allen always knows which question to ask, how to ask it and how to resist being overcome by uncomfortable truths. His skill is eloquently writing step by step in such a way that big issues are fully illuminated and the way forward is clearly lit. It gave me tremendous pleasure and support to read each essay and then puzzle to myself how and why he had 'got it right'. Getting it right is Garth Allen's achievement. Had it not sounded too general, the title for this book could have been 'rightness against risk'.

Of course, six sets of specialists will relish the chance to debate their field with such an open and well informed writer. Behind them generalists, educators proper, will find a hope with hard muscles, a courage to criticize and be criticized in equal measure.

Colin Fletcher
Professor of Educational Research
University of Wolverhampton

October 1996

Acknowledgements

My thanks are due to Gaye Allen, in particular, for initiating me into the mysteries of autism and for generally ensuring that the high risk that this book would never be finished was not realized; to Rosemary Tromans for a decade spent working together in a productive and convivial way; finally, to Ian Lister, for over 20 years of friendship and professional inspiration.

Introduction

One of the main signs of being a rational human being is to work for the containment of future dangers. The prediction of forthcoming dangers is not only a preoccupation of individuals but also one of the central functions of governments. We want governments to minimize risk and to compensate us if events take an unexpected turn. The current cry for help from people with negative equity is a case in point. We now tend to assume that the technology is in place to offer reasonable assurances that things will turn out more or less as we expect them to if everyone involved plays their part. There is clearly a complicated relationship between the public perception of future risks, the role of risk experts in the assessment of uncertainty and political responsibility for meeting predictions and preventing the unforeseen.

This relationship is historically new in so far as the emphasis used to be on ensuring retrospective help when things went wrong. Now the concentration is on prediction and prevention. A return to the political culture of the minimal state of protection of life, property and nation has been coupled with an emphasis on a culture of risk eradication. Paradoxically, for some, there has been a search for high risk activities in, for example, financial and outdoor adventures, which might put some spice back into life.

Of course, the truth of the matter is that we all know what we want from social life, as we have always done, but we are no closer to getting it. That is, we want social institutions to be simultaneously democratic and efficient, to treat us as decent human beings and to deliver the goods. Neither modernization nor post-modernization appears to have solutions to the bad consequences of industrialization and urbanization. Neither prevention nor an acceptable compensation system seems in the offing whereby these bads are nipped in the bud or, once established, are experienced fairly.

This book is about the processes of prediction, prevention and compensation as applied to educational policies and practices. It is about the dangers of not getting things right, when both individuals and governments suffer the costs of a failure to meet reasonable expectations. Given the state of technology, which suggests that we could get a quality product or service, we regularly feel that we should expect a better deal than what we get. The book focuses on education and is selective, perhaps idiosyncratic, in those aspects of education systems which are examined. The theme of risk is applied to educational topics which have been of interest to me since the early 1970s when I first taught in schools.

Readers searching for a disciplinary base to the chapters will spot the influence of economics more than any other. I believe that economic analysis, or more accurately in the case of this book, economic thinking, can be useful in examining educational development and, of course, economics is very much to do with the analysis of risk, uncertainty and prediction. My starting place for pretty shamelessly being prepared to look at any aspect of education that catches my eye is an interest in economics, a belief in the superiority of democratic political systems and a willingness to worship at the throne of the greatest of twentieth-century philosophers, John Dewey.

Part One of this book is concerned with the risks of making the wrong decisions about what should be taught in the secondary school. In the early 1980s, I was a member of the Schools Council Working Party on Social and Personal Education. When the final report of this group came to be written, a crisis of confidence about the work of the group by the Schools Council led to an outside consultant being called in to write up the work of the sub-groups. My job had been to write the initial draft of the section of the report concerned with 'values'. This draft was severely edited, more or less rejected, and a quite different emphasis offered in the final published report. An interest in values in the classroom persisted and when I came, with others, to put together a book on community education, I took the chance to look again at personal and social education in secondary schools. In particular, to see whether any special sort of PSE should emerge from community schooling. The themes of Chapter 1 first appeared, in a different form, in *Community Education: An agenda for educational reform* (1987) published by the Open University Press, and jointly edited by me with John Bastiani, Ian Martin and Kelvin Richards.

From 1974 to 1977, I worked as the Nuffield Research Fellow in Political Education at the University of York, part of the National Programme for Political Education, directed by Bernard Crick and Ian Lister and funded by the Nuffield Foundation. This research and development programme arose out of a strong concern that the basis of democracy as we would wish to know it was at risk because young people were either unwilling to play any part in mainstream political activity, or, when they did play a part, it was on the basis of ignorance. At this stage, in 1974, political apathy and political ignorance were beginning to be well charted. The aim of the National Programme for Political Education was to establish what it was that young people needed to know, feel and be able to do in order to play an active part in the political life of a democracy and to make proposals for the role which schools could play in promoting this mix of appropriate knowledge, attitudes and skills.

Chapter 2 first appeared in a different form in *Education and Community: The Politics of Practice* (1992), which I edited with Ian Martin, and which was also published by Cassell. The book arose out of a concern to report on how educationalists and workers in the care and health professions who focused on education in their job, and who were unsympathetic to current Conservative education, health and care policies, had managed to avoid the risk of sinking without trace under the stress of coping with what for the contributors to that book was an antagonistic political paymaster. At that time, in the late 1980s, Conservative politicians, including the Secretary of State for Education, were offering visions of a new model army of citizens who would willingly knuckle under and make Britain great again. People were the problem rather than structures or processes, and people needed to be revitalized through being remoralized. A briefly popular role model, the Active Citizen, emerged from the speeches of John Patten and Douglas Hurd. Chapter 2 is an attempt to assert the political and moral supremacy of the political literacy specification of active citizenship which emerged from the Programme for Political Education of the 1970s over the Hurd–Patten specification of the late 1980s. The risk for me from Hurd–Patten was that teaching was turning into training, education being displaced by indoctrination, rational dissent was outlawed, and the focus of learning was to become aware of one's own inadequacies rather than to understand the nature of political and civil society.

Part Two reflects an attempt to become familiar with the needs of young people at the sharp end of life. I have spent 25 years in the company of people who have a professional or personal interest in the education of children with special needs. In particular, in recent years, there has been a growth of interest in the education and welfare of children with autism. I had begun to look at this with a research student in the late 1980s, particularly focusing on the array of professional ideologies, policies and suggested intervention strategies which different professional traditions bring to an analysis of the needs of the autistic child. This work never got far because the person carrying out the practitioner research moved to a new job in another part of the country. However, I subsequently realized that I really did not know enough about autism to begin examining particular aspects of autism, for example, in my case, an interest in the respective roles and interactions of speech and language therapists, educational psychologists, paediatricians, teachers, and so on. Chapter 3 reflects the beginnings of an enquiry into the mysteries of autism, and is specifically concerned with the role of schooling in the development of the autistic child. This topic sheds further light on contentious themes such as the involvement of parents in schooling, the ownership of the curriculum in state schools and the effectiveness of alternative teaching and learning styles. The major risk elements in this chapter arise from major disputes within and between the experts from the respective professions and the resource implications of diagnosis. Some professionals, pushed both by their discipline and by their paymaster, are anxious not to label any children as autistic. Others, usually supported by the parents of such children, want an autism diagnosis or are relieved when one is made because it puts the behaviour of the child within a limited frame of reference that they can then begin to work at understanding and it defines a legal responsibility on the local education authority to supply resources to match the diagnosis. Educational psychologists, for example, employed by a local education authority, stand the risk of alienating the parents if they do not offer a diagnosis and offending their resource manager if they do. Such ambiguity and uncertainty is unwelcome when the resolution of the dilemmas really makes a difference to a vulnerable person's welfare.

As expected, visiting the world's poorest known country in the autumn of 1994 had significant personal and professional consequences. Mozambican educationalists are working creatively yet pragmatically to reconstruct their education system following the democratic elections of 1994, bravely putting behind the destruction and dislocation of seventeen years of civil war. I have worked with senior educationalists in Mozambique for two years or so on a variety of projects all designed to meet the National Education Plan target of achieving basic education for all Mozambicans. My own project, since it seemed right that I should have a research programme as well as support other people's projects, was to explore the needs of young people who had, in different ways, become victims of political violence.

My political education work in the 1970s at York, encouraged by Ian Lister, had led to an interest in peace studies. Membership of the Steering Committee of a Leverhume-funded peace education project took me to Belfast in the late 1970s where I was privileged to experience and analyse the work of Voluntary Service Belfast, the Peace People and teachers and youth workers in their efforts to both assert and establish 'normality' in Belfast. This experience was, in part, relived in Mozambique and led to the decision to work again on the theme of education, peace and war. One of the main risks in this sort of work is to be too humble, to be overwhelmed by the enormity of the jobs that need to be done and intimidated by the task of establishing the research, monitoring and evaluation resources and strategies that need to go on at the same time. Given the current managerial obsession with 'value for money' in British education, it is becoming increasingly difficult to work on speculative, non-profit activities. Working in countries where the political and administrative infrastructure can change dramatically in an amazingly short time, such that the original agreed terms of the project between all parties involved are dismantled and need rapid restructuring, can create levels of uncertainty which would be traumatic for people used to, by comparison, the 'normality' of British-based institutions and planning processes. Nonetheless, for me, the initial visit to Mozambique, and then subsequent visits to Mozambique and also, in 1996, to Kisumu in Kenya, working with the Aga Khan Education Service, have put a number of dimensions into my work that were not there before and the task now is to find the time and resources to continue the work described in Chapter 4.

Part Three looks inwards at the nature of the institutions where I have spent the majority of my working life. University staff sometimes pluck up the courage to complain about their life. After a series of end of year exam boards where undergraduates were awarded their classified degrees or not, as the case may be, one sensitive soul, a maths lecturer, wrote an anguished note, freely circulated throughout my College, where he expressed his anger and dismay at assessment processes and their outcomes. Chapter 5 is a partial response to the circular, and, again, tries to suggest an academic response to a cry of frustration and a plea for help (I am no counsellor). The enquiry began with a search for literature concerned with academic staff's experience of the assessment process. This became an exercise in negative documentation but did reveal some interesting work on academic stress and strain, which in turn led to a brief review of the broader topic of occupational stress, strain and coping strategies. The argument presented is that staff, irrespective of a contract culture, do care about their impact on other people and usually try to do the right thing – in this case, to arrive at fair judgements about people's abilities. Credentialism has always been (as long as we have had public education systems) one of the four main functions of mass education systems in industrialized and urbanized societies. My early research work with Professor Mark Blaug at the London Institute of Education on aspects of the economics of education led to a continuing interest in the level of confidence we have in the truthfulness of assessment processes and the certificates they lead to. Assessing other people's abilities is a risky business. Despite the opening remarks in this introduction, we do not appear to have the technology which allows us to avoid the risk of wrongly labelling people. Assessment methods and procedures are either too subjective for the students to feel comfortable with, and, moreover, are often too expensive of staff time to please resource managers, or too mechanistic to meet staff needs to exercise reasonable power over their students. What intrigues me are the occasions when, like the maths lecturer, academic staff feel distinctly uncomfortable with assessment methods, procedures and outcomes. When there is considerable uncertainty about what has been done or what should be done in grading students, how do lecturers cope with this?

Academics are curious about the world and have the skills to turn this inclination into programmes of research and teaching. Strangely, there is relatively little interest in the UK in using the disciplines of academic life to study universities and the people who work in them. Some momentum to do this exists at the moment since, after a decade of political demolition and rebuilding of social institutions in the UK, we now have a new breed of political, economic and social organization. Academics have sought the locus of power in the new political institutions, have charted the emergence of consumers and their powers in transforming economic life and have documented the decline of the traditional family, and much more. However, when I was inclined to be slightly analytical in response to the familiar question, 'what am I doing in this place called Higher Education?', I found few studies of universities other than general accounts of the need to plan, develop or reform. There are lots of blueprints around for some preferred system, and, of course, universities are a rich source for novelists, but there are surprisingly few academic analyses of universities as organizations and even fewer studies of the workers who are employed by them. Chapter 6 attempts to show that there are some ways of looking at universities which could capture some of the complexity of how they are and, in particular, could also provide some guidelines for how they should be. The risk here is that as the new managerialism gains ground in higher education in the UK, searching for relevance and efficiency through a contract culture, the students who attend the universities, who are clearly there, in the main, because they have been promised a good time by friends who have some experience of university life, may drop out at even greater rate than they do now. It seems to me that current high drop out rates are less to do with student hardship and more to do with dissatisfaction with the new regime. Clients, such as students and taxpayers, want universities to be sociable places where work is directed towards good causes, including the personal development of the individual, social cohesiveness through a toleration and celebration of cultural and political pluralism, and security, all with the least possible waste of resources. Universities in the UK are still struggling to find a role in all of this.

The logic behind the shape and focus of this book is threefold. First, the book reflects a variety of experiences working in higher education in the UK and the opportunities these have led to. Second, there was a need to range across themes concerning the nature of knowledge, the nature of individuals and the nature of institutions. Third, the importance of getting education right through deciding what it should be for and how it should be had to be stressed through emphasizing the possibility of getting things badly wrong.

Part I

Learning the Right Stuff

Chapter 1

Teaching about Values in the Secondary School: Perspectives from the mid-1980s

INTRODUCTION

One of the major contributions which recent social scientific research has made to our understanding of social structure and social change is to demonstrate that schools are extremely complex social institutions. We now know that to accurately and truthfully describe and account for the way schools are and how and why they have become the way they are is both necessary, because of the importance of schooling in social life, and difficult, because of the intellectual and financial resources required to be confident that something approaching a truthful and accurate account has been arrived at. Sociologists of education have played a major role in this discovery, demonstrating the difficulties of rolling back the reality of contemporary mass schooling for all to see. Paul Willis, for example, in his influential study *Learning to Labour* (1981), suggests that in order to understand the thoughts, words and actions of teachers and students, we have to engage in three levels of analysis.

First, we have to examine the public face of the school, how the school publicly defends its aims, effectiveness and structure. This would mean, for example, analysing school prospectuses, speeches at governors' meetings and speech days, letters to the press, to parents and so on, and through talking with teachers and students to ascertain the ways in which people are willing to describe openly and explain the nature of a particular school as they see it.

Second, according to Willis, we need to recognize that what people are prepared to publicly acknowledge is often quite different from an inner or private reality. This, of course, is much more difficult for an outsider to observe and analyse. The distinction between public and private accounts of schooling identifies a twin rationality. Willis observes that teacher's 'public' justifications for words and deeds often constitute a response to a private demand simply to survive in the most convivial and productive fashion. For example, a head teacher might publicly defend a shift in the timetable from 40-minute periods to one-hour periods in terms of needing bigger blocks of time to allow the use of microcomputers across the curriculum. The private reality for the head teacher might be simply a need to shorten the morning break time and eliminate the afternoon break because he felt that his staff were not able or willing to control students' behaviour during breaks to his satisfaction. Willis is encouraging us to recognize that teachers and students need to maximize their welfare and enjoyment during school hours and, to achieve their aims, will choose those public explanations and arguments which they feel are most likely to be persuasive.

Third, Willis introduces what he calls the cultural or social milieu of the school, the interactions between the school and the general social universe it inhabits, made up of prevailing political, economic and social structures and pressures. He suggests that any case study analysis of schools should take account of the school's social context, of its cultural milieu. This belief, now approaching the status of a universal truth, took sociologists of education into detailed historical studies of schools and schooling and into entertaining accounts of the innermost mysteries of youth cultures and the views about society, and schools in particular, held by parents, prominent industrialists, politicians, moralists and other declared stakeholders in the state of our schools (Baron *et al.*, 1981).

These three levels of analysis are not mutually exclusive but suggest a systematic research process which acknowledges the difficulties of understanding why schools have become what they have and do what they do and also acknowledges the political requirement to understand how to change them. Judgements about schools, for social scientists as well as the majority of the population, are part of a personal ideology or political belief system. There cannot be a completely neutral social account of schooling. Dewey, in his great book *Democracy and Education* (1944), pointed this out fifty years ago: 'The concept of education as a social process and function has no definite meaning until we define the kind of society we have in mind' (p. 20).

What we like about schools and what we want from schools determine and are determined by our views about the sort of individuals we prefer to live with. In particular, whether we believe that people are born nice, and often lose their niceness, or are born nasty, and have to lose their nastiness. Also our views about schools influence and are influenced by our views about the social structure we prefer. In the UK this often becomes reduced to a conflict between a demand for individual freedom of expression and a counter demand for social obedience. The manner in which we deal with conflicts arising out of these long-standing political issues creates the processes and structures which determine any prevailing social context for schools. The general nature of Willis's suggestions for enabling truthful and accurate accounts of people and their relationships and social institutions and their structures is both intuitively and intellectually appealing. Other approaches to describing and accounting for the nature of schools have been developed, of course, and the number of available case studies of state schools grew rapidly after the deschooling debate of the early 1970s (Green and Sharpe, 1975; Woods, 1979; Ball, 1981).

The main theme of this discussion is that people involved in and committed to the development of community schools need to understand certain aspects of schools which have significantly changed during the 1960s and 1970s (and need to be prepared to act on their understanding). Schools have been subject to an intensified public critique which has required a public defence. The direction, form and intensity of this political questioning of the compulsory school has led to the growth and development of educational reforms which share many features with the ideas and practices of the community school but are not necessarily publicly or privately defended in such terms.

THE GROWTH OF PSE IN SECONDARY SCHOOLING

One of the major growth areas in the secondary school curriculum in the late 1970s and throughout the 1980s arose from the influence of the Personal and Social Education movement (PSE). PSE has not only had major influence on the curriculum but affected the nature of the school as a bureaucracy, its rules, regulations, rhythms and rituals. PSE often encompasses activities which have labels such as pastoral care, guidance and counselling, active tutorial work, negotiated learning contracts and pupil-controlled assessment procedures. Arrangements within the school to enable such activities to take place and flourish helped create schools whose internal organization and curriculum changed dramatically and those changes are now part and parcel of the typical secondary school.

There were a number of attempts during the 1970s and 1980s to produce a conceptual framework for understanding significant features of the ideas and practices of the community school or college. The scheme offered by Angela Skrimshire (1981) is built on the premise that the main litmus test for a community school is that it is sensitive to, and takes seriously as 'problematic', its prevailing cultural milieu. She proceeds to create a persuasive conceptual continuum which enables us to make sense of the ways and means by which various types of community school practices have been brought into being. A simplified version of her framework is reproduced, together with brief annotations hinting at the congruence of the Skrimshire continuum with key elements of the PSE movement (see Table 1.1).

There are other reasons for claiming that people working in and for the community school would benefit from a developed understanding of the popularity of PSE. First,

Table 1.1 *The congruence between community education and personal and social education*

Community school	Personal and social education
School-centred	School-centred
School as community	Can attempt to create community spirit within the school through explicit and/or implicit values education
School with strong home-school links	Can enable parents to be part of a contractual relationship with teachers and pupils so that pupils can be managed through behaviour and performance contracts
School with a community curriculum	Can be main vehicle through which pupils learn in out-of-school contexts (e.g., community experience, work experience)
The neighbourhood school	Can become a major source of community funding of school (through fund-raising organized during, e.g., active tutorial work)
Schools for dual use	Can enable a mixing of ages – e.g., through association with mother and toddler groups, the elderly and the physically handicapped
The community controlled school	Can offer pupils the opportunity to elect representatives for an existing schools council or equivalent, or be a focus to get this started
The school as a community development agency	Can increase pupils' understandings of political issues which may lead to local political action
Community-centred	Community-centred

community education staff working in or from community schools often had a teaching commitment and this often required some form of PSE work. Such workers found themselves teaching fourth and fifth year courses concerned with PSE (usually non-examined) or they were engaged in specific counselling and guidance activities with young people. They may have been involved in community service, work experience or careers education. All of these often come within the framework of PSE in the school. Second, the youth service tradition within community education enabled community staff in community schools to be involved in a range of activities which are traditional in the youth service and have been colonized (often without recognition) by the PSE movement. They could have been involved in fund-raising activities, in school trips and in activities which require a residential component (accompanying one of the PE teachers on a residential week at an outdoor pursuits centre) and may have been encouraged to organize playtime activities (e.g. lunch-time discos). Third, one of the traditions of adult education in the UK has been to work with or on behalf of people (mainly working class) who have failed to benefit from compulsory education. Many workers in community schools, influenced by this particular adult education tradition, were easily attracted or were naturally pushed towards PSE because it was often aimed (in the first instance, at least) at pupils who are identified as less able.

How can people working in and for community schooling make sense of the past growth and development of PSE in the UK? Personal and social education in the UK, as far as I know, has not been subject to a major Willis-type analysis or any other type of sustained analysis which has tried to truthfully and accurately account for its popularity and its rapid growth and development in recent years. That is not to say that we have not had a massive interest in PSE. The interest, however, has been much concerned with what it is (philosophers of education), what it should be (moral philosophers interested in education), what it could be (curriculum and pedagogic specialists), and how it could play a part in the revitalization of the British economy through increasing the will to work (politicians and industrialists) rather than how it has been brought to its current state of relative prominence. There are few, if any, secondary schools in England which would publicly admit that they did not have a policy towards PSE.

Richard Pring, in his very informative book *Personal and Social Education in the Curriculum* (1984), offers a personal synoptic account of the phenomenon from the standpoint of a philosopher of education of international repute, but nowhere attempts to specify *why* PSE has grown and flourished. He refers to the HMI Secondary Survey and quotes the following passage without further comment:

> In recent years these major objectives (namely, 'opportunities and experiences that will help their personal development as well as preparing them for the next stage of their lives') have assumed a more significant and conscious place in the aspiration of schools in response to external pressures and to changes in society, and within the schools themselves.   (HMI, 1979, p. 137)

However, one searches in vain in this Secondary Survey, in a chapter on 'Personal and social development' of 35 pages, for any further mention of precisely what these 'external pressures', these changes, within the schools might be. We have no excuse for not doing this – Willis and others have shown the way. Given the lack of theoretical and empirical attention paid to explaining the PSE movement, the best we can do is to engage in some speculation about the findings of an *imaginary* substantial research effort into the origins and growth of PSE in schools in the 1980s.

We do know a little about the nature of those pressures and changes which had a general impact on public images of schooling in Western society. Husen (1979) broadly characterized the 1960s as a period when formal education, as a universal 'good', was hardly questioned. Any problems in educational systems were to be cured by expansion. The 1970s, for Husen, were a period of less public deference to the legitimacy of major social institutions, such as schools, factories and families. A greater willingness to question the purposes and effectiveness of schools existed among greater numbers of people, some of whom had learnt from Illich (1969) that formal, mass, publicly controlled schooling was neither inevitable nor desirable. The 1980s, Husen rightly predicted, would be characterized by retrenchment, a fear that too much critique and too much change cuts out too much of the good and too little of the bad.

Shor, in *Culture Wars* (1986), primarily concerned with the USA, confirms Husen's prediction. He calls the 1970s and the 1980s the period of the 'conservative restoration'. Within this period, he distinguishes three major episodes of reaction to the liberal 1950s and 1960s. The years 1971 to 1975 were the era of careers education, the beginnings of a freshly articulated demand to improve the fit between school values and skills and industrial values and skills, prompted and professionally controlled by a new brand of teacher, namely the trained and respected careers educator. Shor's second episode, from 1975 to 1982, sees a shift in emphasis through the prominence of a 'back-to-basics' movement, a revitalized call for schools to stand publicly accountable for failures to achieve minimal levels of literacy and numeracy for all their students. The period from 1982 to 1985 he describes as a 'war of excellence', a crusade against mediocrity with a corresponding obsession with new criteria for achievement and for new forms of assessing it. Shor's thesis, in brief, is that the USA, in the early 1980s, witnessed a conservative backlash against liberal, progressive movements in schools and a re-emphasis of vocational, centrally controlled education. There was also, in his view, an attack on the wastage of egalitarian educational principles and policies and their replacement by new forms of student, school and teacher differentiation in order to provide families with greater freedom through greater choice of school and greater rewards for individual merit. The analysis rings true for the UK as well as the USA.

So far this chapter has made three general points. The first is that there are no easy ways of arriving at defensible explanations for major changes in the structure of public sector education in the UK, although social scientific research methodologies have progressed sufficiently to enable such tasks to be undertaken, given adequate intellectual and financial resources. Second, it is assumed that no systematic account has been given of the recent origins and growth of PSE but that this demands to be undertaken both for its own sake and for the lessons to be learnt from such an account by other educational reform movements, such as the community school. Third, it asserts that many of the general descriptive and explanatory frameworks advanced by writers such as Husen and Shor helped define the most fruitful areas of enquiry, at least in the initial stages, for teasing out the truth about the reasons behind the growing popularity of PSE in secondary schools in the UK in the 1980s. PSE has not come about by default or by chance. A 'botch-up' view of school structural change and curriculum development will not suffice.

PSE has grown and developed in certain ways rather than others because of the determined beliefs and actions of individuals and groups who wish to influence what schools do, how they do it and with what effect. PSE has been supplied because of demands for it. These demands can be filtered through Willis's three levels of analysis. From within schools, teachers and students both publicly demanded and defended PSE and privately accommodated it and benefited from it. From outside the school, the prevailing social context, the cultural milieu, provided sufficient conditions to demand and encourage its growth. The following analysis speculates about the specific forms which such demands for PSE have taken. These demands, collectively, represent a coalition of interests. In a pluralist model of social and educational change, such demands would, in principle, eventually lead to counter-claims and demands, to critiques of PSE and to radical or deviant forms of PSE. What counts as radical PSE must be discussed at some other time, although I shall briefly allude to this question in my concluding remarks. The following ten sets of demands seem to me to be intuitively plausible – they ring true, they are what I suspect would be discovered. The list is not exhaustive and is not rank-ordered in terms of importance or chronology. However, they have been simply grouped into demands from 'within the schools themselves' and into demands arising from 'external pressures and to changes in society'.

The demands of academics

Academics in universities and colleges in the late 1960s, especially philosophers of education, were in disarray. They could not agree, nor agree to disagree, about the meanings of such terms as education, teaching and indoctrination (Snook, 1972). They could not agree about which forms of knowledge were most worthwhile and hence offered conflicting advice as to what the primary purposes and characteristics of schools should be. Some nimble academics neatly side-stepped this debate and argued that, anyway, schools were too concerned with knowledge and not concerned enough with promoting the affective domain, with feelings, values and skills (Chanan and Gilchrist, 1974). The broadening and deepening of teacher training from 3 to 4 years in the 1960s and the simultaneous upgrading of the teacher training colleges into colleges of education staffed by a new model army of academic specialists in education, helped create a flow of young teachers into schools who rejected the dominance of the cognitive domain. (NB Now, of course, we have a return to training and school-based training and a rejection of teacher education which may drive out any possibility of a critically sympathetic critique of schools by teachers.) PSE is much more concerned with values education and with the development of interpersonal skills and became a major avenue within schools for offsetting this cognitive emphasis. This shift gave academics in education departments a new lease of life and simultaneously enabled a smooth transfer of power over the curriculum to HMI and its successors.

Teachers' demands to be less authoritarian

One of the major public controversies about teaching and teachers has been the degree (either too much or too little) with which teachers coerce their students to think or act in ways which the students would not freely choose to do. Teachers of the humanities, in particular, again in the late 1960s and 1970s, were increasingly concerned with the quality of their personal relationships with their students. They searched for a shift away from the authoritative and authoritarian, no longer seeking to intellectually monopolize their students' opinions nor to politically dominate students. Such teachers were influenced by the interest in the late 1960s in new forms of political relationships in society, culminating in the community politics movement and also in the deschooling movement, which briefly flourished in the early 1970s and which itself grew out of this more general political movement (Lister, 1974). Teachers demanded to work more democratically, to be less inflexible and predictable, less expert, and to work with students (and with other teachers) within a less autocratic regime.

PSE offers teachers the opportunity to develop a non-authoritarian pedagogy. PSE requires that students and teachers are prepared to get to know one another as people in order to diagnose respective strengths and weaknesses, needs and demands. Full-frontal, teacher-dominated talk and action, as a teaching style, has only a small part to play within PSE. These shifts, from content to process and from teacher domination to teacher facilitation, were able to draw on initiatives in the youth service, for example on non-directive learning methods, and created an arsenal of teaching and learning techniques that enabled new forms of personal relationships in schools for teachers and students alike.

The demands of head teachers

An increase in the average size of both primary and secondary schools took place during the late 1960s and early 1970s. In secondary education, this was in response to demographic factors, the shift to comprehensive education, the move to educate boys and girls together and the economics of school building regulations. Larger schools, especially large mixed comprehensive schools, created a major control problem for head teachers, especially for those who had previously been the head of small, single-sex grammar schools. Head teachers no longer felt they could control the institution. They had little or no training in managing complex bureaucracies and little inclination to change their ways of working. If teachers and students were too numerous to keep in touch with, if school sites (often split) were too vast to regularly show one's presence in every nook and cranny, how could head teachers be confident that the institution was working and thriving, and that deviant students (and teachers) would be identified and dealt with?

One answer was to create a sense of community. Large schools needed to be places where people knew the part they were expected to play in order to promote the well-being of the institution. Traditional means of creating organizational and group identification, through school uniforms, prefects, house systems and organized competitive sport, were often unavailable or ineffective because they were not always in keeping with the prevailing cultural milieu. Students in large schools must be trusted to work through and for the institution without constant surveillance. They must feel part of a community, part of a collective interest which preserves and promotes the school. Such a control mechanism required a major shift in values for some young people in order for them to put the collective interest above, or at least on a par with, self-interest. PSE can and did confront the question of values in education directly. It can and did encourage students to rationalize their words and deeds in terms of their own current and future welfare and enjoyment and in terms of their personal impact on other people, groups and institutions. PSE can and did create the institutional solidarity which head teachers demand. It makes deviant behaviour more noticeable, more difficult to rationally defend and more difficult to continually sustain. This applies for students and teachers alike.

The demands of LEA officers

Civil servants, despite the messages of radio phone ins, do not often set out to deliberately antagonize people. They seek to minimize conflict, not create it. Those LEA officers still in post want to remain the confidant and friend of all members of the local authority education service. A demand derived from this arose during the period in the late 1960s and early 1970s when many secondary schools changed their image and organization.

Many teachers were angry and disillusioned with the extent and pace of change. Many felt they would lose out in any major reorganization. LEA officers were often the target for public abuse and personal bitterness. Large comprehensive schools were often formed by the amalgamation of two, sometimes three, schools, one of which was often a grammar school. Senior teachers in the secondary modern schools often failed to get the senior academic posts in the new school, rarely becoming the new head teacher or one of the senior heads of a subject group or faculty. Senior teachers who could see themselves losing out through reorganization put pressure on LEA officers to create new schools with a sufficiently large senior management team to accommodate themselves within the new school in a position of rank and substance. These could not be academic posts – they were reserved for grammar school staff or for newly imported energetic graduates.

Many local authorities created new schools with a new hierarchy within them, publicly rationalized in terms of protecting the individual welfare of students in a large organisation, but privately defended as a response to pressures from disaffected, experienced teachers. Posts with titles such as Head of Pastoral Care, Head of Counselling, Senior Careers Teacher, Senior Mistress, Girls' Welfare and Community Tutor were offered to re-deployed, low-certificated staff, where loyalty and experience appeared to be more important than academic credentials. Such teachers were often from the same working-class background as the majority of the students they were to work with. Ex-grammar school staff and new, bright graduates were released from the drudgery of actively making the institution work and were able to get on with the task of teaching the brightest and oldest students in the smallest classes. PSE enabled local authority officers to cool out the fears and anxieties of senior teachers during secondary reorganization. It met the bureaucratic demands for conflict resolution.

The demands of students

We now know that for many students, school represents a series of interlocking exchange relationships. For example, teachers offer knowledge, students exchange deference; teachers offer certification or the prospect of a job, students offer effort. Such exchanges, or trade-offs (so much knowledge for so much less bad behaviour) take many different forms and degrees both within and between schools. The 1970s, as we have seen, have been characterized as a period when, in general, there was a significant loss of public faith in the effectiveness of secondary schools. This was true for students too.

For significant numbers of students, especially less able students, existing exchange relationships weakened or disappeared altogether. For example, unconvivial learning arrangements were no longer traded for the prospect of a good testimonial and reference. An increasing number of students resented the traditional authority of the school, an authority challenged by teachers too and recognized as difficult to enforce by head teachers. Students demanded the freedom to impose their own culture on the school, to have recognized the fact that they were individuals with rights to a democratic and productive environment (Hall and Jefferson, 1976).

PSE has put into practice a demand for alternative reward systems (e.g. through records of achievement and personal profile schemes). It stresses the need for a shift in responsibility for action away from teachers and on to the shoulders of students, recognizing and utilizing their demands to be more self-aware, more self-determined and more adult. Furthermore, PSE allows students to do more of the things in school that they want to do, for example talking amongst themselves, engaging in role play, game and simulation, watching television, and making unaccompanied visits out of school through community and work experience programmes. More important, PSE allows students to do fewer of the things they *do not* want to do in school – study written materials, hear teacher-dominated talk, and keep quiet and sit still for the majority of the time. For many students PSE represents a new freedom to negotiate a new series of exchange relationships and, moreover, the possibility of negotiation with teachers from an explicit position of equal strength, or better.

The demands of parents

Parents generally do not welcome major changes in public sector schooling unless such changes are seen to be directed at improving the competitive position of their own children. Parents compare their own children with other people's children who they know and are happy if their own children achieve their expected place in the queue for rewards which schools offer. The school fails in parents' eyes if children do not match up to parental expectations of achievement judged against the achievement levels of other children who constitute the reference group. PSE offers the promise of a new deal for the parents of predicted low academic achievers. PSE meets parents' demands (as well as students' demands) for their children to be treated as individuals, to be distinguished from the group and mass of children, to be recognized as having particular attributes and abilities which need to be identified, nurtured and rewarded no more or less than those of other children.

Moreover, PSE offers parents an explicit invitation to join the teachers and students to make a triangular partnership, a learning contract, for individual students. PSE, through its pastoral care and counselling work, can enable parents not only to know more about schools, teachers and their own children, but also to become active participants. Behaviour and achievement contracts, whereby teachers and students agree on set targets for quality of work, amount of work and time for completion, are one of the hallmarks of PSE. Parents can influence the terms and conditions of such contracts in many PSE programmes. Such intervention roles allow parents to play a direct, purposeful, systematic part in improving their children's current and future welfare through helping their children to reach those minimum achievement expectations, and better.

The demands of economists

Education systems have frequently been cited by economists as a major cause of the failings of the UK economy (Blaug, 1971). Whenever there is a heightened feeling of comparative economic decline and crisis, major critiques of public sector schooling re-emerge in more intensive or new forms often led by economists, especially right-wing economists (see the many critiques of the mass, public school system in the UK published by the right-wing think tank, the Social Affairs Unit). From the early 1970s, the UK economy was thought to be performing very much worse than its major competitors. One of the scapegoats became the size and distribution of public sector expenditure, especially on education and the welfare state. Educational expenditure is an obvious target for cutbacks in public expenditure because of its size – it makes up a significant proportion of public expenditure so any cutbacks in educational expenditure will have a significant impact on public expenditure as a whole. Similarly, increases in educational efficiency and reduction in 'wasted' expenditure will improve general public sector efficiency and help minimize public sector waste.

Another scapegoat for economists became the personal qualities of young people queuing or failing to queue for a job. The former were seen to be lacking in the qualities that the owners of economic resources wanted and, moreover, placed too high a price on their own labour whilst the latter were seen to prefer a life of idleness and state dependency. Schools had to become more cost-effective, creating more productive people at lower real costs. PSE helps meet both of these demands. First, PSE lowers the internal costs of schools (Cummings, 1971). For example, space on the timetable for PSE has often been found by restricting the science and modern languages curriculum even further for less able students; young, cheap teachers have been encouraged to make sure that PSE is part of their workload, and the predicted better behaviour of less able students throughout the school, as a result of PSE, has reduced the costs of all teachers spending significant proportions of their time dealing with disruptive students.

Teaching students how to behave becomes centralized through PSE, which avoids the inefficiency of an often unsuccessful decentralized system, operating in all classrooms with varying degrees of success. Secondly, PSE raises the quality of young people in the eyes of potential employers. PSE has provided a high-profile, centralized, controlled system of certificated character building which teachers, students and parents can more easily sell to prospective employers. Its stress on values education, institutional identification, rational decision-making processes and its behaviour and achievement contracts, have offered students the possibility of offsetting low or zero academic certification with scholastic good conduct medals. The claim is that PSE has helped in the economic war against our economic competitors.

The demands of industrialists

This is a special case of the demands of the economists. Industrialists are offered a major public subsidy through the selection and certification process of schools. Schools offer industrialists a filter which enables them to choose which young people to consider employing and what position and level to employ them at. A major part of the costs of production for any company is labour costs. A major cost of labour is finding the right type in the right place at the right price. Schools offer this service and employers only pay to the extent that they pay state taxes (they, of course, employ their brightest recruits from the education system to advise them on how to avoid paying such taxes).

However, the 1970s witnessed industrial disillusionment with this service. Leading industrialists publicly harassed the Prime Minister of the day with stories illustrating their lack of trust in the school system's ability to identify, promote and reward the qualities industrialists required. They wanted minimum levels of literacy and numeracy parcelled within the appropriate character wrapping. This disillusionment with schools led to industrialists increasingly introducing their own diagnostic tests and devices to offset the high costs of searching and failing to recruit the right sort of employees (they often, of course, decided to stop employing young people altogether, preferring married women on part-time contracts to carry out what traditionally had been young people's work). This meant that industrialists began to bear a higher proportion of the costs of hiring and promoting labour at a time when they were simultaneously claiming that profits and long-term investment programmes were being squeezed by high labour costs.

A quick retreat from such a new burden could be expected. The Manpower Services Commission (MSC) came to the partial rescue by introducing Youth Opportunity Programmes (YOPs) and the one year and then two-year Youth Training Scheme (YTS), all of which acted as a publicly funded selection service for companies. Within formal schooling, PSE offers industrialists more productive workers, workers who know their own minds, have initiative, are used to working to achievement targets and, at the same time, know the meaning of loyalty and social responsibility. PSE also enables employers to be much more particular in their selection procedures than an array of CSEs, GCSEs or GNVQs or lack of them, plus character reference, could ever do. For example, teachers who, through PSE, know the strengths and weaknesses of their students so much better than they ever did before, passed this information on to potential employers when they believed it was in their students' interests to do so. Students produced highly detailed accounts of themselves, through continually monitoring their own aspirations and achievements through various accounting systems, such as personal profiling. Work-experience courses, frequently developed within PSE, allow industrialists to assess students at minimal cost to the firm and, more importantly, allow them to assess cheaply the school as a whole. Some firms cut their labour search costs by avoiding school-leavers from some specific schools altogether. They choose not to consider any students from one school because of a bad experience with one student on work experience from that school.

The same was true for the careers officers representing a public service which was part of the selection and certification subsidy and which, through often being invited into school within the auspices of a PSE programme, would work even more effectively for industrialists (and, let it not be forgotten, for students too who could be more efficiently cooled out of particular job aspirations, thereby reducing their own job search costs). PSE meets industrialists' demands to maximize profits and to sustain the long-term survival of the firm through providing a new way of cutting still further the costs of selecting and grading labour (Broadfoot, 1984).

The demands of politicians

Just as schools are seen to revitalize a declining economy, they can also be viewed as preventive medicine for the ailments of a decaying moral order. The symptoms of the decay are vandalism, in the early 1970s, together with anti-nationalism in the late 1970s and early 1980s and drug related, car and shop-lifting crimes in the 1990s. Schools are seen as both the cause and the solution to social problems, problems which are seen to upset the stability or achievement of a desired political culture. Since 1979, this new political culture has meant a search for a revitalized international political voice in world affairs, achieved through creating a 'strong' economy, itself determined by encouraging people to engage in individual initiatives with energy and gusto, but only through initiatives which support the achievement of international prominence through economic strength. People-building is a major explicit function of PSE. Within a government controlled and financed system, such as mass schooling in the UK, any people-building exercise will inevitably be conditioned in a major way by contemporary power holders, governments and government sponsored and protected institutions. PSE, with its emphasis on a self-examination of the role of the individual in society, becomes the main form of civic education, helping the establishment of the new civic culture, a culture which reflects a new conservative ideology. PSE, in the UK, meets the political demands for a conservative retrenchment both within schools and within the broader social structure.

The demands of the bishops

Religious education, as is well known, has a special status in secondary education. There is a legal requirement that schools ensure that all students experience some form of religious education. The precise shape which this education should take has always been one of the more public controversies about the aims and methods of secondary schools. Debates about religious education correspond to the general social context of religion and morality, and, in particular, reflect the state of health of organized religion in the UK. Interestingly, there is always the possibility of strong arguments for an extension of religious education in order either to arrest the decline of organized religion or to reflect its growing strength.

Knowledge about religious life is made available in schools through religious instruction or religious knowledge courses, religious assemblies, and guest speakers and special events. A shift to the broader idea of morality and moral education, beginning in the mid-1960s and growing in strength throughout the 1970s, created not only new possibilities for student learning but also associated problem areas. What sort of moral education was appropriate? What was or should be the relationship between moral education and moral development? Can, indeed, morality or virtue be taught or can it only be caught from saintly teachers? (Warnock, 1979).

PSE offered a partial solution to the bishops' demands to maintain the strengths, upheld since 1870, of the historic relationship between Church, state and mass school. PSE often encompasses moral education (if not religious instruction) and many of the teachers working on PSE courses have been trained as religious instructors (RI) or religious educators (RE). PSE can be interpreted as part of a reaction by governing elites to the observed and projected problem of a decline in religious interests and activities and a linked decline in the quality of family life. Head teachers have encouraged the growth of PSE, and the involvement of teachers trained for religious instruction work. Such teachers are seen as a necessary member of a PSE teaching team in order to offset, in the head teachers' eyes, the dangerous moral relativism that the media reported was characteristic of youth cultures and of too many teachers in the UK. PSE can and has become a major system for the preservation or revival of virtue. PSE highlights the idea and practice of moral standards.

CONCLUDING COMMENTS

This discussion has argued that PSE became such an important part of public sector secondary schooling that this growth demanded explanation. It has further been argued that people concerned with community schooling are, in different ways, involved in PSE and should wish and be able to make sense of it. Some tentative suggestions have been advanced, anticipating, in general terms, the outcomes of a major, rigorous enquiry into this growth. An equally important associated question is whether we welcome this growth or not. How do we make judgements about it? Do we believe, for example, that the catch words of PSE – self-respect, personal autonomy, self-actuation, independency and interdependency – can be taught within government-controlled institutions in such a way as to maximize real freedom and social justice for the greatest number of people? Do we believe that PSE offers a significant beneficial reform of schools? Such questions may not be answered conclusively by any type of major research programme. People will make their own judgements based on their reading and their experience filtered through their own political belief system. One of the great strengths of PSE is that it may be the major curriculum vehicle for ensuring that all students experience a political education. If, however, we dislike and disagree with the nature of the civic culture which is being produced and reflected through PSE in schools, the dominance of PSE as a political educator within school becomes its greatest failing.

This analysis of PSE reflects an ambivalence which, for me, also cuts across many developments associated with community schooling and with community education. The community school can be thought of as a very appealing prototype for the school of the future. Its concern for peoples' needs rather than institutional growth and survival, for power sharing and empowerment rather than authoritarianism and disenfranchisement and for the cost-effective distribution of public resources, identifies principles which attract many of us to the community school. However, the community school has not and need not lead to the identification and implementation of such principles. Such principles, are, in any case, distractions from real policies and practices and Ian Martin (in Allen and Martin, 1992) draws our attention to Tawney's writings on the British dislike of principles. We need to identify the principles, policies and practices by which the school is to be judged. For me, the key test for the community secondary school is an examination of the arrangements it makes (and fails to make) for personal and social education. The youth service has already been cited as one educational sector which, at its best, far outstrips the school in the care and attention it has paid to social education. In many local authorities, community education simply means a management structure which brings (or attempts to bring) the youth service, adult education and, less frequently, community work together. In such cases, the possibility of a politically powerful and educationally effective personal and social education for young people seems strong and its neglect would be inexcusable.

The ten demands for PSE all produce pressure for change in the same direction – for more PSE. However, these demands need to be related to a detailed account of the forms in which PSE has arisen in the secondary school and public justifications for such different varieties. PSE can, at worse, become a vehicle for repression, keeping both students and teachers in line with a general authoritarian school ethos, or for liberation, allowing learners to explore and identify existing and new forms of personal and social knowledge, skills and values through democratic teaching and learning styles.

We face the general welfare policy dilemma of unintended outcomes – liberation for some can result in repression for others. We may also have to accept second-best positions, where, for example, the outcome is liberating but the intention repressing (true of some YT schemes where young people learnt that they did not have to actively search for dead-end jobs, that to become one of the deserving poor was not necessarily a worthy objective). Such awareness of the double edge of educational policies and movements is one of the prime lessons for the community educator. Moreover, it means that such awareness or sensitivity must be applied when considering whether to invest scarce public resources – for example, the time and budgets of community educators considering initiating or supporting specific forms of PSE. We know that one of the major everyday difficulties facing social workers, community workers and youth workers is how to choose which client or client group to work with or on behalf of. Such decisions that are made should be explicit and, if demanded, publicly as well as professionally defensible rather than unacknowledged and unaccountable.

A secondary school which decides to 'go community' should begin with social education. It should choose those forms of social education which meet the principles already identified (liberating, focusing on people's needs, democratic and cost-effective). It should also choose policies and practices of social education which are fair. This is not the place for a sustained analysis of what we might mean by fairness in the distribution of public resources. However, it seems to me that a politically literate (Allen, 1979) community educator could effectively defend a PSE programme of activities which follow a Rawlsian (Rawls, 1972) principle of social justice. This would be based on achieving fairness through assessing the impact of social policies in terms of their degree of beneficial impact on the worse-off members of the community to be served. This would not mean a 'ghettoization' of PSE. It would mean that all learners in the secondary school would receive the genuine opportunity of engaging in PSE, a policy which just might raise the status of PSE (it suffers from an identification with poor and 'problem' students and teachers) and help identify and create the sort of secondary school many of us would prefer. The community secondary school should be in the front line of this movement, working from principles and taking policy decisions which reflect a political sensitivity to the prevailing cultural milieu. What is pragmatic must and can be good!

REFERENCES

Allen, G. (1979) 'Researching political education in schools and colleges'. *International Journal of Political Education*, **2**(1), 67–82.

Allen, G. and Martin, I. (eds) (1992) *Education and Community: The Politics of Practice.* London: Cassell.

Ball, S. (1981) *Beachside Comprehensive.* Cambridge: Cambridge University Press.

Baron, S. *et al.* (eds) (1981) *Unpopular Education.* London: Hutchinson.

Blaug, M. (1971) *An Introduction to the Economics of Education.* London: Allen Lane.

Broadfoot, P. (ed.) (1984) *Selection, Certification and Control.* Brighton: Falmer Press.

Chanan, G. and Gilchrist, L. (1974) *What School is For.* London: Methuen.

Cummings, C.E. (1971) *Studies in Education Costs.* Edinburgh: Scottish Academic Press.

Dewey, J. (1944) *Democracy and Education.* New York: Free Press.

Green, A. and Sharpe, R. (1975) *Education and Social Control.* London: Routledge and Kegan Paul.

Hall, S. and Jefferson, T. (eds) (1976) *Resistance through Rituals.* London: Hutchinson.

HMI (1979) *Aspects of Secondary Education in England.* London: HMSO.

Husen, T. (1979) *The School in Question.* Oxford: Oxford University Press.

Illich, I. (1969) *Deschooling Society.* London: Penguin.

Lister, I. (1974) *Deschooling: A Reader.* Cambridge: Cambridge University Press.

Pring, R. (1984) *Personal and Social Education in the Curriculum.* London: Hodder and Stoughton.

Rawls, J. (1972) *A Theory of Justice.* Oxford: Oxford University Press.

Shor, I. (1986) *Culture Wars.* London: Routledge and Kegan Paul.

Skrimshire, A. (1981) 'Community schools and the education of the social individual'. *Oxford Review of Education*, **7**(1).

Snook, I.A. (ed.) (1972) *Concepts of Education.* London: Routledge and Kegan Paul.

Warnock, M. (1979) *Schools of Thought.* London: Faber.

Willis, P. (1981) *Learning to Labour.* Aldershot: Gower Press.

Woods, P. (1979) *The Divided School.* London: Routledge and Kegan Paul.

Chapter 2

Education for Modern Citizenship

INTRODUCTION

In the 1980s, the UK subjected itself to intense national criticism fuelled by the anguish of perceived economic and moral decline. The political and popular response was to affirm this decline and seek its resolution through reinventing perceived successful decades as Golden Ages, as images of an ideal present. Individuals such as Richard Branson, Princess Diana and Sebastian Coe became virtuous role models. Other countries, Japan and Germany in particular, were held up to reflect the social and private benefits which accrue to well-regulated hard work and ambition. This soul searching is a major outcome of collective and individual political opinion. Political consciousness, its form and degree, is largely determined by opinions about how well-off we feel we are in relation to our views about how well-off we deserve to be.

This chapter aims to show how causes and solutions to social issues manifest themselves in the UK through examining the debate about Active Citizenship in the late 1980s and early 1990s, its role both as a flashing red indicator for the British disease and as a rallying cry for the rectification of past and present ills. One of the dominant images to emerge from the Conservative Party in the late 1980s was a model of human virtue enshrined within the term 'Active Citizen'. The former Home Secretary, Douglas Hurd, told the Conservative Party Conference in October 1988 that 'the game of dodging responsibility, of passing the parcel of blame from one group to another, simply has to stop'.

Whatever happened to the Active Citizen? So asked a *Guardian* reader in April 1990. He might well ask. These buzz words of the late 1980s have seemingly disappeared without trace. However, I would like to propose that there is a process of evolution whereby the Active Citizen of necessity frequently becomes or should become (a major distinction) a dissident citizen. The clearest example of this was over the question of the poll tax, which brought violence back on the streets and the Tory Party to the brink of defeat in the early 1990s.

Taking responsibility for one's own actions and their consequences is an aim of education which many have subscribed to. In what ways and to what extent, if any, should moulding this Active Citizen be a priority of present day education? The argument which follows is that central government has confused the distinction between education and indoctrination (Brennan, 1981) by allowing one image of the Active Citizen to emerge and to dominate public discourse. This, as we shall see, is one example of the dangers of majority rule since the legitimacy of such propaganda has been located in the ballot box or in the public mandate given through four consecutive 'votes of confidence' for a single party government. An alternative image to the AC (Active Citizen) will be introduced, namely the DC (Dissenting Citizen), and the thin but vital dividing line which exists between the two will be traced.

New Right ideology underwrote the reaffirmation of national strength, identity and pride. Mrs Thatcher's personal achievement in reaching world statesmanship reflected the degree of success achieved in meeting this overriding goal of political strategy. Avoiding the negation of this success – actual or perceived economic decline – has been largely achieved through a remoralization of the British people so that they believe they will have what Mrs Thatcher claimed they have always wanted, freedom to be significant wealth producers for themselves and their families.

The dismantling and dramatic restructuring of the public sector economic and welfare states, criticized as neither seeking nor achieving efficiency and accountability, derive their initial strength and gather momentum from the popular ballot box applause for the model of human virtue underwriting such goals and policies, writ large as the Active Citizen. National progress has frequently been charted as a victory for classes or groups who have wrested concessions from the State to create an increasingly extended and enlightened society. The State has accepted a responsibility for ensuring that its people are not debarred from Active Citizenship through being poor, ill, ignorant or apathetic. The New Right claimed that this paternalistic approach represents restrictions on human freedom because it transfers income or services to people who, as a result of being brought above the level of destitution, become the slave-like dependants of the State.

Active Citizens are free citizens but within a clear, strict moral order. Active Citizens will not be truly free to take responsibility for their own actions unless the State guarantees that they will never be called on to support individuals or causes which no human – rather than saint – would reasonably be expected to support. Active Citizens are to be free from the forced requirement to transfer resources, via the State, to the undeserving poor. The proper, restricted role of the State is to enable free market forces to work unfettered by restrictive practices and to enable Active Citizens to accumulate wealth and to monopolize other scarce experiences – fresh air, clean beaches, great opera, museums and art galleries and even soccer matches. The State is reducing its economic interference to the minimal level necessary to ensure this. At the same time it will do as much as needs to be done in order to ensure that the emerging army of wealth creators, free from the dead hand of public ownership and legal and financial regulation, will willingly dispense some proportion of the fruits of their new freedom and wealth to the deserving poor. The welfare state has to be rolled back, restructured and targeted towards enabling the moral obligations of charity, philanthropy and altruism to break free from the suffocation of State paternalism. Active Citizens will take increased responsibility for wealth creation to produce simultaneously a stronger nation and a stronger economy, bonding people together within and between families in a new moral order. This was the vision.

Neil Acherson has identified a nasty underside to Active Citizenship (*Observer*, 10 October 1988):

The neighbour who writes anonymous denunciations to the police; the passenger who draws the guard's attention to another passenger who might be travelling first class on a second class ticket; the French concierge who tells a returning husband about the men who visited his wife; these are active citizens who exist in all countries. Active citizens provided the Gulag Archipelago with much of its population.

Should we create an educational environment which matches the kind of society Douglas Hurd had in mind when he promulgated the virtues of Active Citizens? John Dewey (see page 4) would not, I suspect, have followed the Hurd instinct, nor followed Mrs Thatcher. Mrs Thatcher, wrote Peter Kellner (*Independent*, 17 October 1988) was:

engaged in the political equivalent of genetic engineering redefining the words we use to define Britain's political landscape, a breathtaking venture, as important as cutting taxes or privatising utilities.

Active Citizens could be passive citizens who uncritically or unintentionally subscribe to the only vision of human virtue recommended.

Citizenship is to do with belonging, to becoming a member. Membership of a nation is paradoxically seen as the legitimate stamp of individuality, in particular, being British. Our citizens abroad – soccer supporters, tourists, overseas sales managers – expect their 'British-ness' to be acknowledged, and, if necessary, put into battle as a counter to the laws and conventions of other countries. However, the concept of British-ness must be susceptible to continuous review and reformulation within a genuine representative democracy. Freedom of speech and association, principles of one-person-one-vote and constant countervailing power, require the possibility and assume the probability of dissent. Images of Active Citizens in a healthy and genuine representative democracy should proliferate and the resolution of conflicts arising from alternative preferences concerning the good life should be an essential function of government. Governments must reflect a majority version of the good life but, in contrast with totalitarian states, this majority version must not be imposed on a de-politicized, uncritical electorate.

THE BRITISH DEBATE ABOUT ACTIVE CITIZENSHIP, 1988–1990

The Concept

Douglas Hurd, when Home Secretary, developed the Tory commitment to define citizenship in 1988 as a policy ploy to defy Opposition attempts to equate conservatism with material self-interest. The concept contains a vision of citizens as those people who, if unshackled from the paternalistic welfare state, would freely engage in acts of altruism, philanthropy and charity. Voluntary and charitable organizations would flourish and reveal people's true nature, their natural empathy and concern for others. This vision also served to offset Mrs Thatcher's oft quoted remarks concerning the absence of society. Active Citizenship offered a reinterpretation of this claim, stressing that processes of mutual aid are doomed to wither away if these are imposed and over-regulated by the State.

In May 1990 John Patten, then Home Office Minister of State, reaffirmed the positive rather than negative role of the Active Citizen image (*Guardian*, 21 January 1990):

To argue that the active citizen is a by-product of a prosperous community troubled by its conscience is patently wrong. Voluntary work, concern for a neighbour, and simple human kindness are not driven by exchange rates, money supply or mortgage interest rates. To suggest that they are is to turn a blind eye to known facts about charitable giving and volunteering. It is also to assign a spurious importance to the economy as a determinant of behaviour. Active citizenship has already fired the imagination of many people and I am convinced that the 1990s will see this develop into a powerful third force in our country. In my view an active citizen is someone making more than a solely economic contribution to his or her community, someone who not only cares but who also acts on their caring instincts.

Mr Patten developed the idea further than Douglas Hurd. Patten claimed that the private sector ought to see the emergence of 'Active Businesses'. These businesses would support voluntary work through secondment of staff, promote volunteering on in-house pre-retirement courses, write cheques for charities and sporting activities and generally be aware 'that their responsibilities extend beyond their immediate workforce to the community'.

Mr Hurd also frequently returned to this theme. In 1989, in a speech in Honiton, Devon, he introduced a further elaboration, the concept of 'good stewardship'. This notion was directed towards those responsible for the delivery of public services and was itself derived from the theme of a 1989 address to the Audit Commission by John Major, then Chief Secretary to the Treasury. The common political concern was that Conservatives should not be portrayed as hostile to efficient public sector providers. The role offered to doctors, head teachers and police superintendents by Messrs Hurd, Patten and Major was that these welfare state professionals cannot avoid direct responsibility for the moral stance of people in their care – the buck stops with them.

Active citizenship remained part of the Conservative Party lexicon with no strong counter proposition currently available. Two distinguished academics and social commentators and activists, Sir Ralf Dahrendorf and Professor David Marquand, analysed this 'big idea' of Active Citizenship (*Guardian*, 1 and 15 August 1990). For Dahrendorf, citizenship is a system of rights or entitlements, constitutionally guaranteed to all members of society. These rights should be social, political, economic and legal. This concept does not sit easily with market forces which accentuate the 'Two Nations' division, as Marquand also points out, 'creating an under-class cut off from political participation by social deprivation'. Rights, of course, for Douglas Hurd, are only legitimated if matched by duties. Indeed, this is another dominant layer of meaning within Active Citizenship. Both Dahrendorf and, though to a lesser extent, Marquand, are appalled by this formulation. As Dahrendorf (1990) says:

> There is something extraordinarily unpleasant in the spectacle of well-heeled Thatcherites or Reaganites egging their leaders on to further attacks on the worn fabric of global entitlement on the grounds that much is heard of rights these days and not enough of duties.

The Active Citizen, for Dahrendorf, is a feature of totalitarianism since the obligations are those of a loyal and dutiful subject acting out a single political image. Active citizens do not have obligations to the preservation and extension of rights, obligations which, according to Dahrendorf, are a feature of free citizens of a democratic state. Robespierre, Stalin and Pol Pot would happily live with the Hurd–Patten concept. More recently, it seems appropriate to equate the emergence of a big idea such as Active Citizenship with the growth of political and religious fundamentalism in the UK. Paradoxically, fundamentalism is an assertion of the right to be different.

Political consciousness

What are the dominant political values in modern Britain? The ultimate success of any attempt to establish a political system based on icons such as the Active Citizen or universal citizenship (as with Charter 88) depends upon the extent to which the moral climate for a new culture of citizenship can be created. How do values such as the enterprise culture, moral vigilance, voluntary obligation, civic virtue and a 'sense of community' fit with what people actually believe in?

Richard Rose and Ian McAllister (1990) suggest that there are new forms of value groups which replace the older divisions of right and left. The right is split between those favouring a free market in everything other than sexual and family morality and nationalism, and those they call a social market group who retain a major role for the welfare state. The left divide between hard left and soft left. All share a role for state provision and welfare values but the hard left is also against institutionalized authority (in the school, home and through the police). Rose and McAllister argue that voters now cluster into nine different value groups:

Traditional

Muck-and-brass welfare		England alone	Strong defence	Victorian Right

Modern

Hard Left	Soft Left	Anti-nuclear Centre	Conservation of environment	Social market

Left	*Right*
←	→

Some people seem to be well on the road to Active Citizenship. In a survey in January 1990 of the values of young people aged 16–24, a survey which suggests how quickly attitudes may have changed since then, seven distinct groups were identified (Euromonitor, 1990):

1. 'Life's a party' (20 per cent of sample). Enjoyment seekers, Tory voters, lager drinkers with little ambition and less social responsibility. A hangover from the 1980s, they are racist and anti-homosexual and are concentrated in the 18–20 age group in the south-east.
2. 'Safety seekers' (18 per cent). Labour voting but middle-of-the road, with unexceptional tastes and habits. Notably nervous of flying and of using the Channel Tunnel, they are prominent in the 22–24 age range in the Midlands.
3. 'Outsiders' (18 per cent). The remaining idealists, they are alienated from authority and incline towards Labour or Green politics. With low income, they buy their clothes from market stalls and, despite claiming to live for holidays, take few of them.
4. 'New moralists' (14 per cent). Austere, cautious and clean living, they are against drinking and smoking and in favour of keeping fit. One in four would vote Green. Likely to live alone.
5. 'Authoritarians' (14 per cent). They are bigoted and aggressive. Two in three are women and they include the highest proportion of supporters of the Social Democratic Party. Pro-police, they drink gin and tonic, vodka and Malibu.
6. 'Greying youths' (8 per cent). Middle-aged before their time, they prefer cash to cheques or credit cards, are keen on marriage and would rather spend an evening in front of the television than go to a concert. Pro-Labour, they are numerous in the 22-24 age group in Lancashire and Yorkshire.

7. 'Young moderates' (8 per cent). The softer face of the 1990s, they are pro-Labour, family-oriented and more celibate than any other group. With low incomes, they buy clothes from catalogues and like cycling.

Educational policy

Another survey, by the School of Education at the University of Leicester, examined citizenship education in 455 secondary schools. This survey was funded by The Speaker's Commission on Citizenship, set up under Speaker Weatherill in 1989. The main conclusion drawn from the survey by its Chairman, Mr Maurice Stonefrost, was that: 'Young people are leaving school without a clear idea of their rights and responsibilities as citizens' (*Guardian*, 21 January 1990). A submission from the Commission was made to the National Curriculum Council. The main approach appears to have been to arrive at a standard syllabus (given the wide variation in citizenship studies shown by the survey) governed by a definition of citizenship. The concept, as elaborated at a February 1990 citizenship conference addressed by the Prince of Wales, is deceptively broad. It included caring for relatives as well as a willingness and ability to join controversial single issue campaign groups. However, a feature of the Commission's work was its interest in and insistence on young people having the opportunity to complete a nationally recognized community service course. There is already, of course, extensive charity fund-raising in schools as well as community service and public service work experience programmes (see below).

Further unanimity about citizenship education displayed itself at the February 1990 Speaker's Conference. The Education Secretary, Mr John McGregor and his Labour Shadow, Mr Jack Straw, both agreed that pupils should be *trained* in citizenship. This training should include the teaching of individual duties and responsibilities (no mention of Dahrendorf's rights), respect for the law and training to understand how society works. Neither, I suspect, would want pupils to serve an apprenticeship with Bruce Kent, Arthur Scargill or Edwina Currie.

These views exist within a broader and deeply divided debate on education policy. Current educational policy is derived from broad conservative themes (not all exclusive to the Tories) such as teachers and local government being the problem rather than the solution to raising educational standards and claiming that the low educational standards of teachers and pupils is the cause of moral and economic decline. Of particular importance to the story of Active Citizenship was Mrs Thatcher's personal involvement in the evolution of a standard history syllabus for the secondary school core curriculum. Her stress on English history, facts and progress seems derived from and limited by the Hurd–Pattern visions of citizens as *de facto* political and moral fundamentalists.

Volunteering

We now know quite a lot about people's views on voluntary work and volunteering. Indeed, surveys by Mori Poll and Social and Community Planning Research (Volunteer Centre, 1990), suggested that the 1988–90 drive to promote Active Citizenship may well fail (as it did) to deliver because of the crucial importance of voluntary – that is, free – activity within the concept and the apparent negative image of voluntary work. Volunteers are still seen as Richard Briers-type characters, namely middle class, middle brow and meddling where they are not wanted. People tend not to volunteer because of the fear of being pressed to do more and more, because it costs them money to do so and because they do not like asking other people for money or goods.

The Prince of Wales is a well known advocate of volunteering. His National Volunteer Force, established in 1990, offers people aged 16–24 the chance to participate in voluntary projects. The government gave £50,000 pump priming money to it. Its central idea, according to the Prince, was to encourage people to mix together for a joint purpose. These Charlie's Angels were to be funded largely by Training Schemes, employers, the Prince's Trust and the voluntary sector itself. Young people in work, in education or on the dole were to be encouraged to spend 12–18 weeks full or part time on projects including helping the disabled, elderly and mentally handicapped. The Prince hoped that the scheme would give its participants a new sense of community (displacing the old or filling a void?) and guide potential which might otherwise be misdirected. The 'life's a party' group were not amongst those few who signed on.

Calor Gas was in on the Active Citizen hype. It sponsored an award organized by the National Federation of Women's Institutes who planned to find the 'Citizen of the 90s'. The panel of judges included WI Chairman, Jean Varnam who, in a press release (*Western Evening Herald*, 2 February 1990) explained the WI's reason for launching the competition (open, incidentally, to women and men):

> This new award highlights our role as a dynamic organisation addressing the social issues of the 90s as we celebrate 75 years of WI service to the community at grassroots level. Citizenship plays a vital part in combating the pressures placed upon communities by the ever increasing pace of modern life. As a community-based organisation we believe it is time that a major award scheme recognised those unsung heroes who make such a valuable contribution to the lives of so many in this country.

This competition is but one feature of the spread of volunteering and its role in the restructuring of local government and local services. 'Active Businesses', as we have seen, may well control the agenda of voluntary groups (Calor Gas over the WI?) as a direct result of funding voluntary groups. This funding may well go to largely uncontroversial bodies, such as the WI, the NSPCB and Telethons. This will reduce funding to less glamorous voluntary groups (Shelter, Gingerbread, local Family Centres). What is happening is that the voluntary sector itself is fast becoming inseparable from the new private sector culture, and the introduction and growing influence of the British National Lottery is cementing this relationship. Hurd–Patten Active Citizens would be equally at home working for Shell or Oxfam in Nigeria. In both organizations, management and public relations issues have displaced consumer sovereignty or human needs as the main decision-making forces.

Trickle-down wealth

Should poor people support the establishment of a New Model Army of Active Citizens? European Commission research (1990) indicated that the number of people who blame poverty on injustice has almost doubled since 1976. Some 70 per cent of people believed that national governments were not doing enough to help the poor and 41 per cent agreed that the poor had 'almost no chance'. The Commission polled a sample of 12,000 people in the twelve EC states. There were 50 per cent who said they would be willing to give up 'a little money' to help the poor (*Guardian*, 5 June 1990).

Active Citizens would be wealth and income maximizers who would then freely (rather than involuntarily through progressive taxation) choose to disperse some of their resources to the deserving poor. In the EC survey, when asked which of two statements best reflected their view of society, 80 per cent chose 'the rich get richer and the poor get poorer', whilst only 12 per cent opted for 'there is less and less difference in income between the rich and the poor'.

Even health authorities in the UK were having to appeal to trickle-down theories of resource redistribution. The *Guardian* (19 April 1990) reported that the West Sussex Health Authority appealed to local residents and businesses for basic revenue finance. A charitable trust was set up in Worthing, to be administered by the Woolwich Building Society, to help the 1700 patients in the district who had been waiting for over a year for their operations. This was the first time a health authority had appealed to local residents and businesses for basic revenue finance. This shift arose directly out of Mrs Thatcher's oft quoted exhortation: 'When you have finished as a tax payer, you have not finished your duty as a citizen.' The Charities Aid Foundation annual surveys of the level of charitable donations made by individuals in the UK show an average of 10p per week per person in real terms.

In a Commons debate on active citizenship and voluntary organizations in December 1989, it was the Tory MP for Wimbledon, Dr Charles Goodrow-Wicker, who claimed that increased private prosperity (i.e. via tax cuts) must be linked with taking greater responsibility for others. John Patten, in the same debate, once more playing a central role in nurturing the Active Citizen concept, criticized Labour controlled councils: 'I am sad to say that there are areas ... where it is extremely difficult to be an active citizen working in the teeth of local opposition' (Hansard, 1989). Once again, we see the theme of setting people free from collective agreements and organizations in order that they will, through human nature, wish voluntarily to redistribute resources.

POLITICAL EDUCATION AND ACTIVE CITIZENSHIP

Political education in a representative democracy encompasses any educational process which encourages and enables people to understand the personalization of the political in their lives and the politicization of the personal. It enables them to make judgements about the distribution of power and resources and to effect changes in these power and resource holdings if these do not fit a rational image of the good life or of human virtue (Warnock, 1979). Politically educated people would be able and willing in a representative democracy to protect themselves and others from the abuse of power and the associated unwarranted loss of freedoms. They would be able to protect themselves and others from inequalities in the distribution of income and wealth and other valued possessions. The problem with the Hurd–Patten Active Citizen is that it is put forward as the only model which reasonable people would aspire to for themselves and defend as a personal goal for others to achieve. Kenneth Baker, when Education Secretary, made this quite clear in his use of categorical language in a speech at Bolton School, an opting out school, in Lancashire (*Guardian*, 10 November 1988):

> Deploring 'moral ambiguities, 60s attitudes to let it all hang out, and the four-letter word', ... the only four-letter word which 'trendy parents' shrank from using was 'don't'.

He went on to describe social scientists as the:

> handmaidens of a revolution in which concepts of right and wrong have become blurred. There are moral values and concepts of right and wrong which are classless, universal, and essential, and which we can all share irrespective of background, religion, or political belief.

Children, according to Mr Baker, should be taught that it is wrong to lie, steal, cheat and bully; and right to respect your elders, to know that you cannot have everything you want instantly, to take responsibility for your actions. Above all it is right to help those less fortunate and those weaker than ourselves. Social progress, Mr Baker went on, cannot be reconciled with divorce and illegitimate birth rates:

> We cannot, on the one hand deplore the apparent decline of young people's behaviour without, on the other, looking at the conduct of those adults who are responsible for bringing these young people into the world.

Associating himself with Prince Charles's advocacy of human scale architecture and environment, Mr Baker questioned whether he was alone in believing that a return to the more traditional moral and social values would greatly benefit our society.

Any democracy should be able to ensure that its citizens are able to lead autonomous lives of their own choosing as morally responsible individuals. This moral responsibility is learnt through attempting to achieve considered, reflective choices on the type of life to live. Mary Warnock (1979), prior to and in contrast with Mr Baker, argued that schools should timetable periods of silence and reflection. Reflecting needs something to reflect on and a representative democracy, built on the probability of significant political change, should, through its educational system, offer people alternative concepts of the good life. How else are we to ensure that one version is not arbitrarily imposed? Robert Nozick (1974) raised libertarian or utopian thinking above the slur of anarchy and recovered the crucially important claim that utopia exists when we are all free, able and willing to visualize and work to realize our preferred choice of utopia.

Utopian thinking connects with democratic theory at the point where it is claimed that no conception of the good life can be arbitrarily imposed on anyone and no one should be subject to arbitrary interference. Neighbourhood Watch schemes would be seen to be antithetical to these principles. What arguably a representative democracy should have is a range of alternative conceptions of Active Citizenship with the caveat that these can be limited to democratic forms if it is accepted that there is no morally preferable political system to democracy. Education in a democratic society means delineating the features of Active Citizenship which make the concept democratic, accepting that there will be different ideal types and different education arrangements which are congruent with these ideal types. We shall discuss later (p. 114) the problem of the paradox of toleration.

One Dissenting Citizen profile, firmly locked into a representative democratic tradition, was drawn up by the co-directors of the Nuffield Foundation's National Programme for Political Education, 1974–77, located in the twin centres of London (Birkbeck College, with Bernard Crick) and York (Department of Education, University of York, with Ian Lister). The opening paragraph of the first major working paper of the Project gives a clear view of the Dissenting Citizen (Crick and Lister, 1974):

> Many people are not politically literate, perhaps we should *not* say 'politically illiterate'. Some may be politically effective, but that is not quite the same thing: unconscious habits can sometimes make one politically effective, as may in other circumstances fanatical intensity. Or a passive and deferential population, who think of themselves as good subjects and not *active citizens*, or who do not think of politics at all, may for some purposes pose few problems to the carrying on of government. But 'political literacy' involves both some conscious understanding of what one is about in a given situation and some capacity for action.

Bernard Crick was adamant that a representative or liberal democracy requires a citizenry willing and able to choose between alternative political parties and groups. In turn, Ian Lister, influenced by John Dewey's work, emphasized the need to avoid the elitism of the reactionary Black Papers of the late 1960s and early 1970s and the off-putting romanticism and nihilism of deschooling. Lister was concerned about the extent to which schools could be democratic, could teach about democracy and teach for democracy. Both Crick and Lister wished to test the boundaries of tolerance by examining whether an educational theory whose goal was the creation of politically active citizens could be implemented in state schools and colleges. Politically literate citizens would avoid slipping into an unconscious deference and would possess the potential for dissent:

> Political literacy must be a compound of knowledge, skills and attitudes, to be developed together, each conditioning the other. Knowledge alone was rejected as an object of political education, but so was an unreflective and uninformed participation.

A politically literate person would significantly participate in political life not out of duty but would freely choose to do so. In asserting, specifying and promoting political literacy, Crick and Lister were always clear that they were not 'postulating some universal role or model: different politically literate persons might have a number of characteristics which vary one from another'. Equally:

> It would be wrong to define a politically literate person as someone who necessarily shares the values of Western European liberalism. That would be, indeed, a curious up-dating of the Whig interpretation of history into present day political education. Such views are to be learned as part of our tradition, but they must themselves be subject to criticism; some scepticism must be part of any citizen and of any worthwhile education, and they must not be universalised without the utmost self-awareness, self-criticism and thought for consequences. However, it is clear, at the least, that there are some kinds of political effectiveness which simply destroy the possibility of other kinds of political literacy. Some biases are compatible with a true knowledge of the motives, beliefs and behaviour of others, some not. Functional political literacy may well be imposed and narrowing. All values are not equal.

Within any form of democracy, the Dissenting Citizen would possess the attributes necessary and sufficient to dissent from the imposition of an orthodoxy, to be able to turn the failure of indoctrination into an educational opportunity.

The relationship between democratic theories and political education practices was never fully developed in the published texts and papers of the Project (but see White, 1983). However, the successful application for funding reflected a critique of capitalist elite democracies. Habermas (1988) has argued that the power structure of capitalist economies requires a depoliticized population reinforced by the competitive materialism and welfare state paternalism which 'cools out' potential dissent. The National Programme for Political Education never claimed this form of ideological justification for its existence, that is, to overcome de-politicization, but it did share and use a fear of de-politicization in order to obtain funding. Lord Trend, a prominent Nuffield Trustee and former Permanent Secretary to the Cabinet, subsequently Rector of Lincoln College, Oxford, was dismayed at the political disaffection and low level of interest in politics that applicants to his College displayed. Low turnouts at central and local elections, opinion poll evidence concerning distrust or dislike of politicians and the falling membership of political parties showed that Oxford applicants were part of a general pattern which illustrated the lack of interest and trust in a political system which depended on people exercising their vote willingly (there being no legal obligation) and intelligently. One characteristic of being politically literate would be to choose to vote after due consideration or to choose to create alternative democratic processes and structures. The National Programme for Political Education, an *educational* research and development project, was a major response to the perceived failings of a *political* system of representative democracy and a capitalist economic system. A willingness and ability to engage in political action led the Project team beyond an implied critique of representative democracy into a debate about whether it was possible and desirable to educate for a participatory democracy and to educate through educational institutions congruent with the vision of a participatory democracy (Pateman, 1970). The politically literate person, as an active citizen, would clearly need to be a Dissenting Citizen in order to work for the realization of an alternative democratic political system to representative democracy, and an alternative economic system to capitalism. Is it currently possible to educate *for* dissent as well as *about* dissent?

> A politically literate person must be able to use his knowledge, or at least see how it could be used and have a proclivity for using it, but equally his or her desire to participate must be informed by as much knowledge of what he is going into and of what consequences are likely to follow from his actions as is needed to make participation effective and justifiable.
>
> (Crick and Lister, 1974, in Crick and Porter, p. 37)

The unusual configuration of 'his'/'her' in this statement illustrates the beginnings of gender awareness amongst the authors!

One feature of such an education process is clear – it would be sharply distinguished from indoctrination. Indeed, the training of teachers and youth workers might, once more, have to include courses and experiences which enable teachers to identify indoctrination and suppress it in themselves and deny it in others, that is, a shift from teacher training to teacher education. Indoctrination would be characterized by teaching about images of virtuous people and the good life as if they were the only images available whilst simultaneously ensuring, through controlling the agenda of the lesson, the progression of the course and the salient features of the hidden curriculum, that no counter visions emerged. Clever, sensitive, teachers can enable people to give equal consideration to a range of utopias, including their own whilst leaving the student free. Indoctrination would imprint an arbitrary conception of the good life as if it were a universal truth.

Pat White (1983) has developed the detail of the relationships between education, indoctrination and democracy. First, she claims, we should accept that in a democracy there are no moral experts on the good life for individuals to follow in detail. The only authority is that which clearly rests on the considered, reflective choice of an individual able and willing to reflect on possible lives. She shares with Fred Inglis (1985) the view that educated people would not live in the ghetto of restricted imagination. Politically literate people, we need to add, would be sensitive to the nature and extent of indoctrinatory forces in order to choose whether to turn indoctrination into education. (Not all indoctrination is bad – for example, to indoctrinate to avoid committing certain criminal or dangerous activities might be desirable.)

Second, argues Pat White, we should acknowledge the extraordinary agreement about what counts as human progress. The Dissenting Citizen would be a disturbing concept if it implied continuous dissent. But this is neither necessary, nor likely. The agreement Pat White is referring to is that in liberal democracies, there is the implicit acknowledgement that governments should guarantee those goods and services and freedoms which are the prerequisites for both living a good life, recognizing or imagining different conceptions of the good life, and ensuring that citizens are tolerant of these differences. The absence of poverty, ignorance, hunger and ill health are the necessary conditions which underpin the exercise of political imagination and political strategy. Yet there is the danger that the new Active Citizens would be people who, as never before in post-war Britain, could demonstrate that they deserve their citizenship partly through identifying and clamouring (fuelled by the popular press) for the punishment of dissent. These state guaranteed rights and entitlements to a minimal good life remain only for the deserving Active Citizens. The current buzz welfare policy phrases of 'targeted groups' and 'value for money' reflect the view that Active Citizens, through transfer payments and subsidies and the finance of welfare state institutions and professions, have been trapped by an unfair universal redistribution system which rewards the bad as well as the good.

Procedural values congruent with the moral frameworks of participatory democracies also need to be spelt out. Critics of the possibility of ever realizing a participatory democracy have argued that the concept itself is contrary to human nature – many people, it is claimed, whilst experiencing only the conditional satisfaction of representative government, would not swap it for any other system. This may or may not be true. The Dissenting Citizen would wish to reflect, at least, on the possibility of significant political change. A Dissenting Citizen would have the confidence and feelings of efficacy to override deference, servility and acquiescence. From the past, from other countries or from the imagination would come possible Utopias which would need to be worked out in detail – no small task!

The Crick and Lister (1974) specification of political literacy is quite clear about the crucial although partial role of imagination:

> A politically literate person would also know the kinds of knowledge that he or she needed, and did not possess, in a given situation, and how to find them out. Paradoxically, the politically literate person knows what he or she does not know.
>
> (Crick and Lister, 1974, in Crick and Porter, p. 41)

Bernard Crick (1975) was equally clear about the need for and nature of these procedural values. If there is a genuine political education, certain values are presupposed. These Crick called 'procedural values' for they are not substantive values like various justifications of authority, like equality or types of justice, but rather presuppositions of any kind of genuine political education or free political activity. For one thing, the politically literate person cannot just accept one set of values as correct. They will see that the very nature of politics lies in there being a plurality of values and interests, of which they must have at least some minimal understanding. In paragraph six of Document 1 of the Programme for Political Education these procedural values were boldly and simply identified as 'freedom, toleration, fairness, respect for truth and respect for reasoning':

> I assume that a teacher should not ordinarily seek to influence the substantive values of pupils – and that frontal assaults are not likely, in any case, to be successful. But I assume that it is proper and possible to nurture and strengthen these procedural values. Anyone can see that in real life and politics there are many occasions when these values may have to be modified, because they can conflict with each other, or with substantive values such as religious, ethical and political doctrines embody. Part of political education is to examine just such conflicts. But this does not in any way affect the primacy of these procedural values within a genuine political education. The objection to them is, indeed, more likely to be that they are pie more than poison, nebulous platitudes more than harsh indoctrinatory concepts.
> (Crick and Lister, 1974, in Crick and Porter, p. 41)

It remains to specify the forms of power relationships within which a Dissenting Citizen would wish to flourish in order to create and maintain genuine democratic political systems. The claim is that this virtuous person, the politically literate or Dissenting Citizen, would be aware of a range of power forms that need to be selected before being exercised according to rational thought within the moral framework of the procedural values. Political action, the key educated outcome of political education as we have defined it, requires the defensible use of power. Pat White (1983) argues for an education *in* power and claims that we should recognize that power lies within those institutions which determine the distribution of income and then analyse what income does and does not buy. She claims that within a participatory democracy, citizens would prefer the most egalitarian distribution of political and economic power that was consistent with ensuring an appropriate division of labour. Furthermore, she maintains that citizens would want the state to ensure a level of welfare provision below which no one must be allowed to fall.

White's exercise in guesswork or logic is familiar, though no less important for that. However, the forms of power are still left unspecified through these claims about the preferences of power holders. What forms of power may DCs legitimately use to arrive at this egalitarian utopia, should they choose to work for it? Forms of power can be categorized in many ways (Wilkinson, 1986) including the spectrums of violent–non-violent, coercion–persuasion, education–indoctrination, manipulation–openness, argument–brainwashing. Each of these is itself conditioned by the source of authority vested in the power-holder. Active Citizens are energetic wealth creators for self and family and for nation and community. Community is interpreted as an obligation, derived from celebration of the happiness that comes from material wealth, to dispense charity, philanthropy and altruism to the unhappy deserving poor. The capacity to provide and the need to receive transfer payments and subsidies may be the most significant power relationships of our times, for such payments determine the nature and extent of dependency relationships and thereby define the limits of personal independence and communal obligation, and, hence, freedom from arbitrary interference. The range and degree of altruism available to a society is a crucial determinant of the relationship between private and public provisions and regulations. As Crick and Lister state:

> An understanding of politics must begin with an understanding of the conflicts that there are and of the reasons and interests of the contestants; it cannot be content with preconceptions of constitutional order or of a necessary consensus. A politically literate person will not hope to resolve all such differences, or all differences at once; but he perceives their very existence as politics.
> (Crick and Lister, 1974, in Crick and Porter, p. 37)

The claim must now be directly made that the politically literate person is the Dissenting Citizen who may choose the Hurd–Patten image of the Active Citizen but who would be free to reject it and work for alternative visions of human virtue and the good life. Dissenting people may disagree with a popular or official view. Dissent comes from the prior quality of resistance and a politically literate person would only knowingly acquiesce to any prevailing orthodoxy. We need to reassert the educational implications of the 1970s Programme for Political Education in a form which connects with the immediate future. Current state policies and proposals are stuck together with the super-glue of indoctrination in such a way that the materialist moralists and eclectic elitists of contemporary conservative thinking and the institutional conservatism of new socialism are difficult to challenge.

A right to equal treatment and respect is a necessary condition for the expression of dissent without fear of reprisal or disqualification from civil society. As long as governments legitimize inequalities and orthodoxy, then the educational focus for producing the Dissenting Citizen has to be on education for human rights, as Dahrendorf has asserted. This would at least set the agenda for ensuring the guarantee of minimal material inequalities in primary goods such as income, health, learning and self-respect, a guarantee which the Butskellite consensus of the post-war years acknowledged but failed to deliver, a guarantee which has now been expired for more than a decade. George Orwell, the creator of Winston Smith, is as pertinent today about the danger of totalitarianism as he was in 1945: 'Orthodoxy means not thinking – not needing to think. Orthodoxy is unconsciousness' (quoted in Wrong, 1979).

REFERENCES

Acherson, N. (1988) *Observer*, 10 October.
Brennan, T. (1981) *Political Education in a Democracy*. Cambridge: Cambridge University Press.
Crick, B. (1975) 'Basic Concepts'. Document 3 of the Programme for Political Education. In Crick, B. and Porter, A. (1978) *Political Education and Political Literacy*. London: Longman.
Crick, B. and Lister, I. (1974) 'Political literacy. The centrality of the concept. In Crick, B. and Porter, A. (1978) *Political Education and Political Literacy*. London: Longman.
Dewey, J. (1916) *Democracy and Education*. London: Macmillan.
Euromonitor (1990) *Young Britain: A Survey of Youth Culture in Transition*. London.
Guardian (1988) 10 November.
Guardian (1990) 21 January, 5 June, 19 April, 15th September, 1st September.
Habermas, J. (1988) *The Philosophical Discourse of Modernity*. Cambridge: Polity.
Hansard (1989) H.C. Deb, 4 December 1989.
Inglis, F. (1985) *The Management of Ignorance*. London: Basil Blackwell.
Kellner, P. (1988) *Independent*, 17 October.
Nozick, R. (1974) *Anarchy, State and Utopia*. Oxford: Basil Blackwell.
Pateman, C. (1970) *Participation and Democratic Theory*. Cambridge: Cambridge University Press.
Rose, R., and McAllister, I. (1990) *The Loyalties of Voters: A Lifetime Learning Model*. London: Sage.
Volunteer Centre (1990) *Voluntary Activity*. Berkhamsted.
Warnock, M. (1979) *Schools of Thought*. London: Faber.
Western Evening Herald (1990) 2 February.
White, P. (1983) *Beyond Domination*. London: Routledge and Kegan Paul.
Wilkinson, P. (1986) *Terrorism and the Liberal State*. London: Macmillan.
Wrong, D. (1979) *Power, Its Forms, Bases and Uses*. Oxford: Basil Blackwell.

Part II

Children at the Front Line

Chapter 3

Autism and the Education of the Young Child

INTRODUCTION

The term autism first appears to be used by Leo Kanner in 1943. It comes from the Greek word *autos*, meaning 'self' (Baron-Cohen, 1987). Kanner saw children at his clinic who appeared shut off from the social world and inhabited a private world closed to outsiders. How had the children come to be like this? After a history of research, which Baron-Cohen refers to as blind alleys, we now know that the child with autism may have impaired cognitive development, which leads to a failure to process information in a socially appropriate way. For example, a child with autism may put in what appears to others to be extraordinary efforts to complete a trivial task, and may generally have a different set of priorities for choosing, say, things to remember than any one else in his family (autistic children are predominantly boys).

Autism appears to be characterized by the child failing to make judgements about social situations, or other people's intentions and emotions and we now know that quite young children are usually perfectly able to connect with their social world and become 'street-wise' in terms of their interactions with other people. Young children, but not young autistic children, can distinguish between the world as it is and how it is represented by people they interact with. For example, they see a person cry but know, on this occasion, that they are crying through happiness rather than sadness, even though crying is nearly always a signal of distress.

Children with autism are prone to either avoiding social situations or to offering stereotyped responses to situations, both of which serve to distance the child still further from the usual forms of social interaction. In this chapter, the focus will be on schooling the child with autism: can anything be done within the framework of pre-school or compulsory schooling to improve the autistic child's ability to function in a social sense or to take some of the risk out of appearing to behave badly, of seeming to refuse to 'fit in' and the social stigma for children and their families which comes from such behaviour?

PARENTAL ROLES AND UNCERTAINTIES

There are no major schools of thought about how pupils with autism can be educated which do not involve some role for parents. The main focus of this section will be concerned with analysing some of the major approaches that are currently favoured in working with pupils with autism in terms of the type of emphasis they place on the involvement of parents. This analysis exists within a broader debate about the role of parents in the education of children. We need to emphasize the particular way in which proposals and practices for the involvement of parents in working with teachers on behalf of pupils with autism has been established. It will be shown that there has been a lively debate in the UK in the post-war period about the relative roles which the state, teachers and parents should play in being held responsible for the education of the nation's children (Allen, 1987).

It has been fashionable to use the term partnership simply to focus on home–school relationships or home–school liaison and this has tended to hide the fact that there has been a growing body of legislation which tries to determine the ways in which any particular partnership works itself out. Partnerships come in all shapes and sizes and it is not very meaningful simply to assert that some relationship exists as a 'partnership'. For example, the relative power positions of the partners can be quite different from one another, depending on the formal and informal arrangements made. Some approaches to working with pupils with autism are quite specific about the partnership that is implied, or more strongly, the nature of the partnership is at the core of the approach taken. With autistic children, teachers have to be surrogate parents and parents have to be surrogate teachers, and this complex mix of professionalism and amateurism is fraught with the risk that the ingredients will not gel. Autistic children are surrounded by major professional and parental uncertainties about what might be best done with them and for them.

Currently in the UK there is a mixture of provision for pupils with autism. Some pupils will be attending state schools within a local authority policy which encourages a transparent equal partnership between teacher, parent and the LEA. Whilst this may remain an ideal in these localities, given levels of resourcing, at least there is a clear resolution to achieve an equal partnership and this should benefit the education of the pupil with autism. At the other end of the scale is a situation where the nature of any partnership is deliberately made mysterious and may, at worst, serve to cover up a deliberate attempt to exclude parents from any real partnership in the education of any autistic pupils within the LEA's responsibility. The parents of pupils with autism may be unlucky and find themselves in places where the pedagogical need to actively involve parents of children with autism is precluded by the LEA's policy. The local political culture may reject any notion of equality in the educational policy-making triangle of state–teacher–parent. Distributional social justice would mean that it did not matter where you lived, and that parents have rights to fair treatment as far as resource allocations in education are concerned, including resources which enable an appropriate partnership between teachers and parents to emerge and be sustained.

One of the main themes of the 1978 Warnock Report was parents as genuine and strong partners in the education of pupils with special needs. Indeed, a whole chapter, 'Parents as Partners', stressed early intervention. Three principal forms of support were identified which were to facilitate the active involvement of parents: information, advice and practical help. The Elton Report of 1989, *Discipline in Schools*, continued the theme of stressing the importance of parents working alongside teachers. Twenty-five years previous to Elton, the famous Newsom Report can be seen as the post-war forerunner of many educational reports and enquiries which ended up arguing for the need to involve parents in the education of pupils as active agents rather than as passive bystanders. The legal framework for the compulsory education of pupils in the UK is still largely determined by the 1944 Education Act which, of course, put the onus on parents (rather than on the children themselves) to ensure that children attended school and put the onus on the LEA to supply education of a suitable nature for the child. The education of pupils with autism crystallizes the issue of what the relative powers of the recognized partners in the education process should be.

One of the main difficulties in establishing effective teacher–parent partnerships is the clash between what John Bastiani has called professional power and lay authority (Bastiani, 1987). The parents of children with autism experience a range of professional judgements about their child. These diagnoses come from GPs, paediatricians, speech and language therapists, audiometricians, health visitors, social workers, pre-school advisory teachers, nursery/play group teachers and helpers and educational psychologists. This can lead to different views being offered, a condition of differential diagnosis (Schopler and Mesibov, 1989), which can leave the parent not only confused and distraught but also powerless. At best, the parent diagnosis is considered alongside the other views so 'lay authority' is recognized to be on a par with 'professional authority'. At worst, the experience of parenting and the parental view about the best interests of the child is totally ignored. Nonetheless, even in the latter case, the parent is still expected to go along with the professional diagnosis offered and to play out the parental role which the diagnosis implies.

The teacher has to be very sensitive to the nature of parental involvement with the child in the home, to the experience that the parents have had with professionals so far and to the expectations that the parents have about their role in the education of the child. Some parents wish to hand over their child to the 'experts' whilst others claim the label 'expert' for themselves: 'parents possess intimate knowledge of their own child and are the most experienced people of all in knowing what their child can do and what they cannot or will not do' (Andrews, 1992, p. 55).

Andrews, however, is talking about the somewhat rare case in which the parents and, by implication, other influential family members, all agree about what is best for the child. It may be the case that the mother and father disagree about important basic ways of working with the child, such as handling difficult or bizarre behaviour, or they might both agree but a powerful grandparent may question their judgement. The implications of this for teachers is that there may be no one accepted parental view about the child and there may indeed be a series of competing views. So, the most complicated case may be where there is no unanimity within the professional group nor within the parental 'group' about how the child should be treated. The bottom line in partnership arrangements with parents is that the local authority ensures that the parents are given the chance to learn about what autism may be, to examine in some systematic way why their child is the way he or she is. The professionals have to trust the parents as authorities on the welfare of their children and the risks of not doing this are manifold in the distress one sees in the parents of autistic children who feel their voice is never heard.

When autism is diagnosed in children reference is most often made to the 'triad of impairments' (Wing, 1988). This means that the child has problems with communication, socialization and imagination, and parents find it easy to give and relate to examples of these features.

Communication

Parents often notice that something is 'different' about their child (even though, as we have seen, they may disagree about the nature and implications of the difference) at the stage when normal children are acquiring language. There may have been earlier signs of impairment, such as lack of gestures, but these will usually have gone unrecognized by the parents and also perhaps, by any professionals associated with the family. This can lead to a lack of bonding between parent and child which in itself can create difficulties. For example, the child with autism can fail to share a point of interest with a parent through drawing the parent's attention to something. The child needs to be taught to 'touch point' (Christie and Hall, 1993) and the techniques for enabling the child to develop this facility have to be made known to the parents:

> Some parents are fortunate enough to live in an area where a Portage scheme is in operation ... Parents are shown how to play an active part in facilitating progress in small steps towards relevant goals.   (Aarons and Gittens, 1992a, p. 21)

If it is generally accepted that access to a Portage scheme is necessary in order to ensure that it could be called on if deemed appropriate, then the onus is on the LEA to explain why Portage is not being made available. Aarons and Gittens use the word 'fortunate' but this is not something which should be left to chance. Professionals, of course, are put in a well-known dilemma when an accurate and full diagnosis will expose the failure of the LEA to recognize the importance of active intervention in supporting parents who wish to have access to the Portage approach. Equally, where a Portage scheme is made available for pre-school children, the onus is on the parents to ensure they play their due part in the scheme.

Unfortunately, diagnosis may come too late for the child with autism to benefit from this programme. For those children with communication difficulties who would have benefited from a Portage scheme but who missed out, it may be apt for the teacher to initiate a Portage-type relationship with the parents even though the child is now of school age. Touch pointing, for example, may be a suitable technique to establish at the beginning of a teacher–parent partnership irrespective of the age of the child.

Socialization

All children are different but children with autism attract attention because they are clearly not the same as other children whose individual differences are well known and, therefore, accepted. Moreover, where there are other brothers and sisters, the behaviour of the child with autism is such that they are immediately distinguished from their close relatives. Parents cope with this 'high profile' child in various ways, some through not coping at all, some through protecting the child against social exposure, some who try and treat things as normal, and some who have a worked out strategy based on either a policy arising from discussion solely within the family or in collaboration with salient professionals. The social and political context in which the child with autism finds themselves is clearly extremely important. For example, if the child is brought up within a family and a neighbourhood in which differences in race and gender are seen as a richness rather than as a source of conflict and competition, then the recognition and toleration of people who are 'different' is much more likely to exist. This can set a community context for the child with autism which, at this macro level, is beneficial. Here, yet again, we cannot avoid the political issue of the difficulties in establishing a tolerant and empathetic culture which for autistic children, like other children but more so, is necessary for their inclusion in society.

One child with autism has severe temper tantrums when he is not allowed to remove tins of custard powder from the shelves of the supermarket. What are parents to do in this situation? A number of strategies are available. One is never to take the child to the supermarket. Another is to allow the tins of custard powder to go into the trolley and arrive home. Clearly, neither of these is acceptable if the emphasis is on normalization and the freedom to be a full member of civil society.

Discussion with professionals about what to do in this sort of situation has to exist within a culture of sharing of ideas. The professional as expert, as sole authority, is not always an appropriate source for reaching a solution because there may be no purpose-built solution waiting to be picked off the theoretical shelves. What needs to be done is for the parents to have a forum in which they can check out their views about how the supermarket visit should be handled. This raises the associated issue of how to establish such a relationship with the parents that open, productive and convivial exchanges of information and ideas can take place. Strategies could include implementing:

- home visits
- parent workshops/coffee mornings
- parent support groups
- provision of a parents' room
- home–school notebooks
- establishing a resource base of books, etc.
- encouraging, where available, the use of audio and visual recordings of the child

Phil Christie (1993) has described how teachers should be active participants in the establishment and maintenance of home-based projects. For many teachers, the resource framework within which they work does not allow teachers to be facilitators in the ways recommended. In reality, many children with autism find themselves within a class or group which has children with a variety of special needs. Therefore, the dilemma for the teacher is to have a parent partnership policy which is broad enough to enable and encourage a set of purposeful teacher–parent liaisons yet, at the same time, is specific enough to meet the needs of the parent of the child with autism. One of the well documented tendencies of the parents of these children is to share an equally intense obsession with professionals about the child (Jordan, 1990a). This can lead to a cosy feeling of solidarity between teacher and parents, possibly fuelled by a joint concern for the transparent vulnerability of the child. However, it can lead to the exclusion of other parents of children in the class or group and to accusations of special and hence unfair treatment and, at worst, may destroy or inhibit the growth of partnerships with these other parents.

Imagination

Philosophically, it is not entirely clear what imagination is, yet, notwithstanding this conceptual problem, it still remains apt to claim that the child with autism seems to have too little of this elusive quality to make them 'normal'. Lack of imagination is characterized by the way in which this special child may play. A car is usually played with through copying the way in which cars are observed in the real world. Cars, in play, are propelled along imaginary roads, stop at traffic lights, and get petrol at petrol stations. The child with autism, is likely to do things when 'playing' with the car that are rarely seen or reasonably imagined – the car may be upended, wheels spun, and watched and watched for what seems to be an unusually long period of time. The concept of 'boredom threshold', used by the manufacturer of toys, has little meaning in the market-place of autism. Role play, of course, is seen by child psychologists as essential to normal personal and social development, where the child works out its own identity and its preferred relationships with others:

> Failure to engage in rich role play situations is not only a reflection of the pupil's difficulties but also leads to further difficulties; the pupil misses valuable opportunities to take on the role of others, to act out emotions and events and to learn all the social and language skills which go with these activities.   (Jordan, 1990a, p. 15)

Parents and teachers need to agree on ways in which these essential activities can take place such as to promote the child's normalization. This may mean that the child has to be directly taught to role play, for example, and role play must not be allowed to take place only as a result of the child's inclination or choice since it may not ever happen in a way that is educationally valuable. One useful breakthrough is the insight offered by Frith (1989), who works with the phrase 'theory of mind'. For Frith, an essential state of normalization is to be able to predict what other people are like and how they are likely to behave. Part of rationality is to be able to predict other people's thoughts and actions. For the child with autism, this facility to link bits of information in such a way as to create a way of understanding themselves and others is lacking. This also means that the capacity to learn from experience is limited. To describe the intellectual make up of the child with autism is simultaneously essential yet fraught with difficulty and uncertainty. For example, there is an understandable tendency for the parents to highlight the child with autism's 'islet' of ability, to see the development of this as intellectual progress when in reality it offers no evidence at all about general intellectual growth. Professionals, of course, may equally delude themselves because all are desperate for signs of improvement. What is not desirable is for parent–teacher partnerships to be built on the quicksand of false expectation and optimism, yet somehow some faith in the prospect of mutual benefit from the partnership must be sustained: 'Unless claims for successful treatment can be supported by objective evidence, parents and professionals should continue to remain sceptical and wary' (Aarons and Gittens, 1992, p. 53).

Establishing faith in the partnership is undermined by the difficulty of coming to a diagnosis that all partners are able to accept totally. It is, therefore, understandable that there is a tendency to search for 'miracle cures' since the blinding flash of this sort of revelation may be the one thing which all partners can coalesce around. More usually, the process of coming to an agreed way of working with the pupil with autism will be a mixture of trial and error and pick and mix. Alternative treatments currently on offer include:

• Holding Therapy: where, to cure premature independence, parents insist on comforting their child.

- Higashi – 'daily life therapy': emphasizes regular, vigorous physical activity, including a stress on intensive instruction in music and visual arts.
- Option Approach: children receive intensive and loving one-on-one stimulation from a rotating series of teachers, all trained by the child's parents, in a specifically designed playroom.
- Facilitated Communication: starts from the view that the child's difficulties in communicating are rooted in neurophysical and emotional problems and technology, such as a word processor, is used by a facilitator to guide the child in his efforts to communicate.
- TEACCH, a broad programme of activities, first introduced and developed in North Carolina, USA (Schopler and Mesibov, 1989).

What is needed is some agreement about the relative strengths and weaknesses of these approaches in general and then how aspects of one or more of these approaches can be rationally locked together so that all partners have an agreed role. The National Autistic Society is currently promoting just such a situation but it does mean that the Society itself has to be open-minded and continually review its recommended approaches. Otherwise, it simply becomes just one more source of expertise rather than a forum for the identification and dissemination of the costs and benefits of all known potentially beneficial treatments. For example, one parent was convinced that the Higashi school in Boston, Massachusetts was the only school which could offer her son John the intensive therapy needed to overcome his eating disorder. This involved fund-raising, securing money from Dyfed LEA and persuading the school to offer John a place. We are not told whether there was a queue for places at the school and, if so, how pupils' needs were prioritized. The Higashi approach is not now exclusive to the Higashi schools and pupils might meet Higashi-inspired treatment, such as a stress on physical education, in a variety of settings. Dyfed had no specialist facilities for pupils with autism so there was no possibility of pick and mix or trial and error. The Local Authority had, at that time, to enter into negotiations with the parents for treatment outside Dyfed. Many accounts by parents of the search for treatment does suggest a system of trial and error, searching for somewhere or something which might help. This can lead to episodic treatment which counters the need for stability. Parents need the costs of trial and error to be taken out of their lives through receiving appropriate professional advice about their children or what else is 'professional' to mean?

Teacher–parent partnerships which facilitate effective teaching for pupils with autism can only arise if certain key features of autism are recognized. The partnerships have to acknowledge the pupil's need for stability, continuity, structure, individual treatment according to need and, by implication, the active avoidance of contradiction and paradox in the child's life. This means that all adults who have an interest in the education of this pupil need to share a common basis in:

- the assessment of the pupil's particular level of functioning and learning style
- deciding on an appropriate scheme of intervention
- establishing a rank order of priorities
- monitoring and reviewing progress

Parents should be involved with teachers at all of these stages and, indeed, at times will be working in the home with the child in exactly the same way as the teacher has worked with the pupil in the school. For example, the use of a common language by both teacher and parent may be essential for the majority of pupils with autism – clear, short unambiguous instructions or requests have to become second nature to the adults involved. We have already seen that such a coalition may be difficult to establish when there are many adults involved, and of course parents vary in the resources, especially time, they can call on to work with their child: 'People, particularly parents, need to say in short sentences EXACTLY what they mean, otherwise autistic people do not stand a chance in normal conversation and it might make them just give up' (Jolliffe *et al.*, 1992, p. 17).

Special interests, obsessions and abilities can be the source of a fruitful liaison for the teaching of academic and social skills. Cooking and eating activities provide a means by which stimulation can be enhanced in such a way that essential skills are initiated and developed. Such skills are also clearly visible, or more strictly, their absence can prove embarrassing for parents in public places, so there is a strong chance that all adults will agree to prioritize working at these activities. Mesibov (in Schopler and Mesibov, 1989) makes the further important point that cooking and eating provide interactive opportunities for non-verbal pupils. Temple Grandin (1986) has written about the difficulties that pupils with autism have in establishing order in their lives and work. Clearly, the onus is on adults to provide the means by which sequence and predictability are introduced. For example, the TEACCH programme enables a particular form of order to be reached through recommending that the architecture of the work environment and the repetition of tasks and activities are always in the same sequence and all utilize visual prompts for the pupil. This not only provides the order looked for but can also begin to empower the pupil through enabling them to get on with their activities at home and at school. At this point of course, divisions between teacher and parent, and home and school start disappearing and the concept which emerges is one where, wherever the pupil is and wherever adults are who have an interest in the child, a common code of practice prevails.

The ultimate aim, according to Jordan (1990a), is to be able to work with the pupil in such a way that they can begin to gain an awareness of the sense of things, that one thing follows another, that actions have consequences, that thought should precede action and that life is conditioned by rewards and punishments. This process of active reflection is something that is very difficult for autistic children to come to. The general problem here is that empowerment for the autistic child is difficult to realize because the child exists outside of reason.

Partnerships between teachers and parents and all other adults with an interest in the education of the pupil with autism remains only an ideal in some localities in the UK. If it is essential that partnerships exist, then they must be part of policy creation and policy implementation. Parents I have met are hypersensitive to variations in the level and type of resource base made available for working with pupils with autism. Even within LEAs there can be inequalities between one region or neighbourhood and the next. These differences can prove to be intolerable and, at worse, can lead to parents being 'invisible'. Paradoxically, for the LEA or other agency which is establishing policies and practices for the pupil with autism, investing in the active, effective support of parents in partnership with teachers may be the only way that the pupil can progress. At the least, the chances of progress are increased massively if the potential contribution of teachers and parents working together in an open, democratic and mutually supportive way is recognized by the powers that be.

WHAT TO TEACH THE AUTISTIC CHILD?

Autism is a life long condition. The school is only one of the agencies within the life span which has a major role to play in the formal education of people with autism. These people have all sorts of needs but the emphasis on the school directs our attention to their educational needs, however broadly conceived. The ability of schools as social institutions to meet the educational needs of any young people must be kept constantly under review but it will be taken as read that schools, as places of compulsory education for children aged between 5 and 16, can be and indeed must be effective agencies for the promotion of learning for all school age children. There is so much differentiation in human beings that any attempt to plan any sort of provision from a basis of needs is fraught with difficulty. This is true of welfare services in general yet there is now, in the 1990s, a strong ideological commitment amongst a variety of professionals to direct their interventions towards meeting people's needs. Professionals, including teachers, who work with autistic children have to feel confident that schools are effective agencies for meeting the special needs of such children because schools are the dominant educational institutions of our times.

The National Curriculum is part of the 1988 Education Reform Act which makes major new provisions and prescriptions for the nature of compulsory schooling. The basis of the National Curriculum (NC) is a statement of entitlement (Lewis, 1991). Children in maintained schools have a right to experience the NC. To withdraw this entitlement requires strong justification. The NC is not automatically disapplied for children with special educational needs (SEN). This means that there is an implied case, at the least, for seeing the NC as the major means by which the educational needs of all school age children are met. If there were a wide range of disapplications, this in itself would destroy the integrity of the NC as a universal, common experience.

The NC was received with mixed feelings by the SEN professional community. One position is: 'If we are stuck with it, we have a duty to our pupils to make the best of it'. Pragmatically, teachers, in collaboration with other professionals, have begrudgingly made the most of a situation that they claim not to have invented. On the other hand, some teachers have claimed that aspects of the NC simply put into place processes which are already common good practice in special education, for example, the stress on assessment (Daniels and Ware, 1990). There are four main elements in the NC:

- prescriptions about preferred forms of knowledge
- specifications of programmes of study
- specifications of attainment levels
- prescriptions for methods of assessment

Some teachers (Wragg, 1989), especially primary teachers, see the NC as a typical example of, for them, the worst sort of educational policy. They claim it is too complex to understand, too difficult to implement, shows a complete disregard for the realities of the classroom and, above all, represents a direct attack on the integrity of the teaching profession since it takes power away from teachers. In contrast, there has always been an undercurrent of feeling, as always, with some truth, that the curriculum of some special schools had been unnecessarily limiting. The prescriptions of the NC imposes an educational menu on all maintained schools. The inclusion of science and technology, for example, as part of the main course of the NC, has been applauded since it means that SEN children have to be offered an appropriate experience of these subjects.

Teachers and professionals, including the SEN caucus, have seen considerable potential in the NC basic framework. The stress on agreed forms of knowledge for all children will increase the move to include SEN children within the general framework of educational policy-making and implementation and practice. The NC has been attacked for bringing into being a whole new educational vocabulary yet, as with the subject base, the emergence of a shared language amongst teachers, other professionals and parents has been welcomed since it allows an informed dialogue to take place (Peacey, 1993). This vocabulary is at its most complicated perhaps in the field of assessment. Yet the stress on assessment within the NC can be claimed to arise out of the good practice of the best SEN provisions. Good practice in SEN has always meant, for teachers and educational psychologists and so on, doing some hard thinking on creating methods for assessing growth, potential and comparison.

The NC was part of the 1988 Education Reform Act ideology which led to changes in the locus of control of schools, taking power away from local government and teachers and giving enhanced powers to central government, parents and to governors. Once more, this new set of partnerships in education could be seen as beneficial to the interests of SEN children since part of the ethos of SEN work, at its most progressive, has been to recognize that teachers cannot and should not work in isolation. Strong home–school partnerships are often at the root of good educational practice and this can be seen time and time again in SEN work. Giving parents a role and, moreover, power, can be seen as part of a growing recognition that all adults are potentially teachers and many adults, as tax payers, have a stake in the quality of schooling irrespective of whether they have school age children or not. It could also be argued that the NC and the public controversies surrounding it have beneficially raised the interest in and the standard of debate about education generally.

Children with autism are very much a minority interest amongst educationalists in general and, oddly, amongst the SEN professional community, at least as indicated by the few citations of autism which occur in popular and recent SEN literature. Autistic people of compulsory school age are to be found in a variety of educational settings. Some are in private schools or institutions which fall outside of the regulatory powers of the 1988 Act. Within the maintained sector, these children are to be found in special schools and units, in schools solely for such children, in mainstream schools with or without ancillary help/specialized teacher support or, exceptionally, at home with home tuition. Potentially, the NC can fundamentally change each and all of these contexts. There are estimated to be 20,000 children with autism in the UK (Connelly, 1990). The majority of these will be in special schools and probably predominantly in Special Learning Difficulties (SLD) schools. Of course, there will be a hidden pool of children with autism found in a variety of institutions who have not, for one reason or other, had their autism recognized.

The main setting, therefore, in which autistic children are to be found where their education is governed by the National Curriculum is the SLD school. The implementation of the NC in SLD schools is the formal responsibility of the governors of such schools. The most severe criticism of such schools in the past, which governors cannot now ignore, is that they practised containment rather than education. What children learnt was less important than how they behaved, or, rather, the main form of learning which took place for teachers and students was how to get through the day as quickly as possible with a minimum of stress for all concerned. This caricature will have, thankfully, less intuitive appeal in the 1990s since the influence of subjects, programmes of study and standardized public assessment will destroy it. For the schools which to some degree used to exhibit the features of the caricature, the shift in ethos brought about by the demands of the NC must have been or will be a substantial culture shock.

The quality of personal and social education work in any school is an important feature of the overall quality of the school. Special schools generally have been noted for the emphasis they have placed on PSE work. Indeed, it has been possible to justify the monopoly of curriculum time with PSE, as we have seen in Chapter 1. Therefore, autistic children in school settings would normally experience a commitment to PSE work from teachers and the degree to which this work has been tailored to the needs of specific children will vary from school to school. Nonetheless, the expectation would be that autistic children stand a good chance of receiving planned, relatively individualized attention through PSE in SLD schools. Indeed, this is essential, given that 'social impairment' (Wing, 1988) is a fundamental aspect of the autistic disability. Higher functioning autistic students in mainstream will not necessarily have experienced PSE in the same way. For example, the introduction of PSE in secondary schools has often been through Personal and Social Development which, as Jordan (1990b), has argued, leaves too much to chance. She contrasts 'education' with 'development', claiming the latter to be too facilitative and too vague to meet the needs of autistic pupils. The NC includes PSE as a Cross Curricular Dimension which is meant to permeate throughout the NC subject areas (Jordan, 1990b). This means that SLD schools have had to rethink the way in which PSE can be introduced throughout the curriculum as well as offered as a discreet subject. Some schools, of course, will have always planned for both of these approaches but the NC emphasis on permeation can take time away from PSE work.

What autistic pupils need from schools is an effective intervention programme which motivates them through turning their special interests or obsessions into productive vehicles for learning. This can only happen if appropriate learning contexts are established. Autistic children must have a high quality programme aimed at developing their language and communication skills. English is one of the core curriculum subjects of the NC (NCC, 1993a). Within the framework for English there are six specific elements, one of which is AT1, Speaking and Listening: 'The development of pupils' understanding of the spoken word and the capacity to express themselves effectively in a variety of speaking and listening activities, matching style and response to audience and purpose' (NCC, 1993a, p. 2).

First reactions to this attainment target suggest that the autistic pupil may never reach this stage since impaired communication is one of the 'triad of impairments' (Wing, 1988), as we have seen. These children have great difficulty in making sense of, and using, all aspects of verbal and non verbal communication. Moreover, attainment across the NC, arising as it does from the culture of a literate society, requires a certain level of language and communication competence which autistic children may never reach. The languages of mathematics and science, both core NC subjects, have their own 'internal' vocabulary which can determine levels of attainment reached in these subjects. AT1 in mathematics, 'using and applying mathematics' specifies:

- Applications
- Mathematical communication
- Reasoning, logic, and proof   (NCC, 1993b, p. 2)

One of the many difficulties facing the autistic pupil is an inability to conceptualize, to see things in the abstract and to see the relationships between discreet fragments of information. So, these children, when faced with the above targets, would find it impossible to articulate their findings and understanding of these findings. They may, of course, be able to show what they have learnt by visual means, to simply do and make things. The use of alternative forms of evidence about learning and their legitimacy within the NC assessment framework is of vital importance to autistic children. To stick too rigidly to a universal curriculum policy does the interests of autistic children little intentional good.

A feature of autism which has already been mentioned but which needs emphasizing in the context of the impact of the NC is a rigidity and inflexibility which conditions the ability to learn. According to Jordan (1990a, A1) this:

> can extend to every area of the child's thinking, language, and behaviour. Examples of this can include ritualised and obsessive behaviour, literal thought, insistence on sameness and difficulties with creative processes.

This has implications for the structure of the total learning environment, in particular the style of curriculum delivery. Bill, a boy of five years old, finds it difficult to turn over the page of his maths book. The contents of the next page are not known and not predictable. Therefore, the act of turning the page is unwelcome even though the actual maths on the new page is usually within his capability. He needs to work with a teacher or parent who recognizes what is going on in Bill's head every time a page needs to be turned. The NC is underwritten by an assumption that common access to learning means common activities, done in common, and this position is not immediately conducive to the needs of children like Bill. Moreover, Bill is in need of regular reflection on the task completed in order to reinforce learning or to clinch the learning. The pace of learning for autistic children will be very different from the majority of children. Bill needs thinking time before engaging with a task, as well as reflection.

Sir Ron Dearing (Dearing, 1993) in his interim report recognized that the attempt to be universal in the 1988 Education Reform Act needs to be treated with caution and with common sense. We have already seen that autistic children are a minority yet, within the entitlement concept, their specific needs as a group and as individuals must be capable, in principle, of being met within the NC provisions and prescriptions. Bill is only one child but all children count. Dearing raised a series of questions about the NC and asked for teachers' views about the best way forward (Dearing, 1993). He defined four major issues:

- How should the breadth of the core curriculum be reduced?
- How should his review focus, by subject or holistically?
- What should happen beyond Key Stage 4?
- The future of the 10 level scale of attainment.

There are currently 19 foreign modern languages which count as NC languages. The Attainment Targets are as expected: AT1 Listening, AT2 Speaking, AT3 Reading, AT4 Writing (NCC, 1993c, p. 2). For autistic children, there is a sense in which all languages are foreign languages. Nonetheless, it seems plausible to suggest that autistic children will have considerable difficulty in accessing modern foreign languages since acquiring and using their native language is so problematic, unless other languages become an obsession. Indeed, it may be that for autistic children, more so than children who do not have such severe difficulties in communication, trying to learn a 'second' language may well crowd out the development of the 'first' language.

The main focus so far has been on primary schooling although the previous discussion has hinted at the extent to which the educational needs of autistic children will be badly served by the NC and its development at secondary level. Autistic children and their parents, like all other families, at root simply want the best education they can get. One major framework for evaluating the effects of the NC is whether it leads to better schools. This seems so obvious to say yet it is too easy to forget the context in which the NC was introduced. This context was an alleged widespread public disillusionment with the quality of education. Falling reading and mathematics standards and a decline in young people's moral standards have been alleged, all of this highlighted through constant comparison with other countries who were supposed to have got their education systems on the right lines for economic and spiritual success. Teachers, of course, were battered by the direct attack on their professionalism. The way in which the attack was made – for example through the publication of policy briefings and consultative documents during the summer vacations – was guaranteed to hit teachers when they were most disinclined to deal with the criticisms and to think through the implications of the indicated reforms. Environmentally friendly teachers were particularly incensed by the number of trees cut down to produce papers which stood little chance of being read! It is no exaggeration to argue that the NC, along with the other elements in the 1988 Education Reform Act, led to considerable anxiety and stress throughout the teaching profession and to early retirements, time off for 'illness' and widespread loss of self-esteem. Nonetheless, teachers, parents, children and educational administrators, together with all the other 'stakeholders' in the education industry, still need to and are still trying to achieve the best possible (or least worst) schooling.

In 1992, the Secretary of State published a review of *Curriculum Organisation and Classroom Practice in Primary Schools*. The Minister wanted to review available evidence about the delivery of education in primary schools (OFSTED, 1992, p. 5). HMI then went on to monitor the reactions of schools to this discussion paper, surveying over 70 primary schools to assess their reactions to the issues. HMI published their own report as a result of this monitoring, *Curriculum Organisation and Classroom Practice in Primary Schools. A follow-up report* (OFSTED, 1992). These two documents offer significant guidelines for creating and identifying good schools. SLD schools within the primary age range sector have, therefore, a recent and authoritative framework for reviewing their practice. The issue here is whether there is anything in the framework which would significantly improve the possibilities of the SLD school being able to more effectively meet the needs of the autistic child within the boundaries of the NC. No special schools were part of the survey and again this raises the fundamental question about how far and in what ways curriculum development, which is aimed at reforming all schools, is an appropriate framework for the reform of particular schools, such as SLD schools, and the special children who will be found in them, such as autistic pupils.

What is needed is for those professionals with experience and expertise in working with autistic pupils to be able to influence the introduction of the NC prescriptions in all the settings in which autistic children are to be found. This is a tall order given the relative scarcity of such individuals, their lack of mobility given a reluctance to fund in-service work and the 'closure' of some schools to any 'outside' advice. One particular problem is that many of the experts work in schools funded by the National Autistic Society and this restricts still further the access of maintained schools to the necessary expertise. The onus is on LEAs, themselves working from an extremely limited resource base, to come up with some creative mechanisms for the dissemination and implementation of good practice. Of course, they may well find it difficult to do nothing at all given the 'voice' of the parents of autistic pupils. My experience has been that schools in the maintained sector are willing to take autistic children if they have appropriate resourcing.

The NC is an 'entitlement' curriculum. It is not only a philosophical or ideological prescription for what children should learn and how this learning should be assessed but it legislates, as never before in central government legislation for the curriculum, in order to remove teacher discretion from the promotion of learning in the maintained sector. The NC's attempt at universalism raises major problems for the learning of children with autism and, if teacher discretion or freedom of interpretation is successfully removed, then the educational experiences offered to autistic pupils may not be what they need. Nonetheless, we do know that there are good schools and we do know that there are sensible frameworks available, for example, from OFSTED, which offer models of good schools. Furthermore, we know that there is a growing volume of expertise within the educational professions which suggests how we can work effectively with children with autism. One person who has done as much as anyone in the UK to develop our ability to meet the educational needs of pupils with autism, whatever the setting, is Wendy Brown, former Principal of Broomhayes School, North Devon. We need to rise to her challenge:

> Given the difficulties it is sometimes really inspiring to see what some schools do achieve but it does not just 'happen'. A great deal of intelligent hard work is required and I believe that much of it will depend on whether the adults involved are brave enough to take charge.
>
> (Brown, 1993; unpaginated)

TEACHING STYLES AND THE AUTISTIC CHILD'S 'PROGRESS'

One of the major causes of enhanced uncertainties in the education and development of children with autism is that we lack research which articulates the children's description and analysis of their own needs. Furthermore, we know that there is a culture of resistance by teachers to the work of researchers, even research done by teachers. For example, research (Jones and Meldrum, 1993) suggests that 1:1 teaching may be a critical factor in effective teaching of pupils with autism. This proposition points to a major dilemma for teachers and practitioners generally. This dilemma concerns the relationship between research and policy and practice. On one hand, teachers are desperate for some evidence about the most effective ways to work with children, a hope that research may throw up something that will indicate effective intervention strategies. Yet, on the other hand, researchers themselves, and academics who filter research through to teachers, couch the integrity of the research in very equivocal terms. Researchers and academics are loath now to use words such as cause and proof since we know that social scientific research, including educational research, is only, at best, an approximation of the truth. Nonetheless, some research is more 'truthful' than others simply because it has been done well and is accessible to practitioners.

The research by Jones and Meldrum is impressive in the sense that the authors manage to give warnings properly about the research being interim, part of a bigger study with an

ongoing life. The main methodological problem facing researchers concerned with the performance of pupils with autism is that they can rarely obtain data direct from the pupils.
Much educational research relies on effective communication between the researcher and the
research population. Where people are of interest to the researcher because they have communication problems, as with pupils with autism, this means that the researchers need to get
the data 'second hand', in the Jones and Meldrum case this comes from significant adults in
the pupils' lives. Moreover, the research is confronted with the well-known problem of taking one independent variable, 1:1 teaching, and trying to establish a relation with the
dependent variable, pupil performance, when we know that there are many potential variables which affect performance. For example, see Jones and Meldrum's finding that pupils
in situations where 'special provision' was available made the most learning gains. This
may, of course, have been significantly influenced by the context in which the 1:1 teaching
took place. Any form of intervention may be more effective in the 'special provision' context. The research itself does not prove that 1:1 teaching causes the augmented learning
gains perceived by the adult respondents and the 'finding' has limited value but it does offer
some evidence about teaching and learning styles appropriate for children with autism.

The Jones and Meldrum study, in its discussion of methods, stresses that much of the
work was with parents:

> Parents' perspectives on the approach being used and its effects on their child make up a
> large part of the information collected. Their involvement in the approach is a key aspect
> of some of the approaches being evaluated.   (Jones and Meldrum, 1993, p. 33)

Here is a clear case where parents are both the judges of performance and key agents
in influencing performance, presumably as contextualizing the 1:1 teaching of the
teachers and themselves practising 1:1 'teaching' at home. The point is simply being
made in this commentary on the research that it is easy to slip from the caution expressed
by the researchers themselves into thinking that the holy grail has been found – in this
case, that pupils with autism will always benefit from 1:1 teaching.

Of course, it seems intuitively appealing that 1:1 teaching in any educational setting
will be the most effective form of teaching. This is simply a confirmation of the influence of the teacher in teaching and confirmation of the notion that the teacher's influence
on one child may be diluted by the presence of other children. Therefore, it follows that
undivided teacher's attention benefits the pupil. This proposition is supported by the
general culture of parent views about their child. They want their child to be noticed and
recognized as an individual and the process of individual teaching is the public face of
due care and attention being given in the classroom. The task which the Jones and
Meldrum study does not address is to get beyond the general feel-good factor in close
teacher–pupil attention and to offer reasons why the claimed gains in performance from
1:1 took place. Indeed, their level of analysis is situated in a well known framework of
what makes for 'good' teaching (see, in particular, Section 3, 'Structure, management
and content of the session' – this reads like a college tutor's comment on a student on
teaching practice or the notes of an OFSTED Inspector). The problem here is that even
where some technique may be particularly appropriate to pupils with autism, such as 1:1
teaching, we may need an equally creative form of analysis to get at cause and effect,
or the reasons for effectiveness in the particular case of pupils with autism.

We can imagine why 1:1 teaching may be more effective than other teaching strategies but these reasons themselves will be determined by our specification of what autism

is and how its behavioural manifestations can be controlled and changed. Indeed, relationships between diagnosis, assessment, teaching and evaluation are themselves conditioned by the specific form of teaching (one stage in the cycle) which is adopted. The 1:1 teaching is in itself a method for diagnosis, assessment and evaluation and it may be that 1:1 is chosen not only because of its effectiveness as a 'teaching' technique but because of the other functions it can serve.

It is possible that 1:1 may be a critical factor because of the very special cumulative effect on learning produced by the 'triad of impairments' (Wing, 1988). Pupils with autism are not only delayed in development but have, according to Wing, specific difficulties in socialization, communication and imagination, as we have seen. Such children experience problems in organization, sequencing, motivation, concentration, flexibility and cannot generalize their learning. They are characteristically obsessional, easily distracted and have major difficulties in making sense of the world. Pupils with autism, it has been suggested, typically demonstrate these traits because, according to Frith (1989), they have an inability to integrate pieces of information into coherent wholes. Frith's school of thought about autism is that people with autism lack a 'theory of mind':

> To identify the core features we had to look below the surface of the symptoms. It was then that we could see the red thread that was running through the evidence. It is the inability to draw together information so as to derive coherent and meaningful ideas.
>
> (Frith, 1989, p. 187)

'Normal' teaching relies on predominantly verbal systems of education and learning. Teachers talk, children listen; teachers ask questions, children answer; teachers set tasks, children carry out the task and, as a result of all of these interactions, learning is said to take place. For the pupil with autism, language has to be specifically tailored to the level of understanding of the children. For example, language has to be unambiguous, clearly historically and socially contextualized and supported by appropriate visual prompts and, on occasion, physical prompts too. Where the context is such that all the pupils are at the same level of functioning, for example all the pupils are autistic and have the same autistic condition, then it may be possible to work with the pupils as a group. Such occasions are rare and, even then, there are other reasons why working with them as a group may not be appropriate. Pupils with autism may themselves not experience the 'group' in the same way as the teacher or non-autistic pupil. The teacher may still need to name the individual or physically gain their attention in order for the pupil to realize that they are being addressed and that they are expected to do certain things.

'Normal' teaching involves social conditioning. Pupils are expected to want to please the teacher, to impress other children and to be part of the group – not to stand out or be different, except, perhaps, if this is to be rewarded. The usual rewards and punishment systems available to teachers do not apply. The 1:1 teaching may enable teachers to individualize the conditions under which learning can be made possible. For example, learning readiness may vary for each pupil, according to the rhythm and rituals of the day. Teachers need to 'seize the moment' in order to work effectively and this demand on teachers to be so sensitive to the pupils' state of being may only be realized if teachers have some capacity or opportunity to stay so in touch with the pupil as to spot the moment. This may, of course, be where collaboration between the teacher and a classroom assistant may be at a premium.

For young children one of the functions of group work or working in groups is that they can copy or imitate the language and actions of other children. The pupil with autism in a group context may not benefit from this learnt behaviour. In this sense, 1:1 teaching is not complementary to group work but may, for some autistic children, be the only way in which they can progress. For example, during physical education, a ring of children will be throwing the ball to one another. They must catch the ball and take a decision to throw the ball to someone else. This may be in turn or they can choose who to throw the ball to but the other child must stand a chance of catching the ball. For the pupil with autism, there may be an immediate problem with their attention to the task in hand or their understanding of the task. If they do not realize that they have to prepare themselves to receive the ball, this not only lessens their chance of catching the ball but possibly antagonizes the rest of the children because the game is 'spoilt'. The autistic child may 'learn' that the game is actually about avoiding the ball, or being hit by the ball. Learning in this context may require someone to be behind the pupil with autism, positioning their hands to receive the ball and directing their attention when the ball is to be thrown, perhaps to them. This can also be reinforced through encouraging, through question and answer, the use of appropriate language, for example, the concept of the 'other', that is, the child who has thrown the ball to them or who they have to throw to. They may also, according to Jordan, need to have the sequence of events gone over with them immediately: 'In this sense the learning does not stop because the task is "complete"; the child needs time and opportunity (and possibly more structured facilitation) to reflect on his or her own performance' (Jordan, 1990, p. 21).

This example shows that there has to be a planned yet reflective relationship between working with the pupil with autism as part of a group and on a 1:1 basis. Again, the sequence of group and individualized work with such pupils may be important. For some children, it may be best to rehearse the activity on a 1:1 basis before exposing them to the group situation and then to reinforce the activity through 1:1 teaching.

Imagination, as we have seen, is the capacity to realize that things can be different from the way they appear. For autistic children, there may be no transfer to a real situation which they have experienced many times – that is, a trip in a car. The 1:1 teaching can be important here if it facilitates the learning of simple rules. For example, if they cross the path of the car being played with by another child, the cars collide – that is, two things can get in each other's way. Board games such as Ludo and Snakes and Ladders are potentially useful since they too stress the need to observe rules, such as taking turns and moving in relation to a given number on a dice, or moving up or down, as in Snakes and Ladders. The 1:1 teaching may be required first in order to establish the rules of the game. This will be important for the pupil with autism so that they can effectively participate thereby making their participation acceptable to other children. The selective use of 1:1 teaching must follow on from assessment even though, as has been argued, the process of assessment itself may require 1:1 teaching.

Working on a 1:1 basis is, of course, a feature of many of the professionals who work with pupils with autism and other children with special needs. These include speech therapists, educational psychologists, occupational and physiotherapists and doctors. The prevalence of 1:1 work in these professional contexts has a number of implications for 1:1 teaching and classroom practices. First, to the degree that the pupil with autism is actively associated with such professionals, the child can become accustomed to this form of adult–child interaction. Given the well-known need (Grandin and Scariano, 1986) for pupils with autism to have continuity and regularity in their lives, this does pave the way for the teacher to work in similar ways to other professionals. Second, the reverse is true – where teachers work on a 1:1 basis, this may pave the way for other professionals to engage with the pupil on their particular 1:1 basis. Third, all of the professionals associated with the pupil need to have a co-ordinated approach. At worst, the pupil may be visited on a particular day by their speech therapist and educational psychologist and that day may be one where the teacher has planned for concentrated 1:1 teaching. In such a case, the pupil may get no social interaction with other children at all.

The degree and type of 1:1 work which the pupil with autism experiences will also vary according to the intervention approach adopted. For example, Holding Therapy makes extensive use of 1:1 work (Welch, 1988). Here, parents use various strategies in order to make 1:1 contact with them unavoidable. The same stress is found within the Option Approach:

> In this type of program, children receive intensive and loving 1-on-1 input and stimulation from a rotating series of teachers (trained by the child's parents) in a specifically designed playroom. The design of this room and program is to eliminate outside distractions so that the teacher's input is received in an optimum atmosphere and is the main attraction.
>
> (National Autistic Society, 1993, p. 25)

Behaviour Modification takes many forms and was first used for children with autism by Dr Ivar Lovaas (Lovaas *et al.*, 1989). In the early stages, the technique was used to reduce inappropriate behaviour but now the emphasis has shifted towards skills development. For example, the maxim of 'first we work, then we play' is commonly in use to gain compliance from the pupil for the work tasks ahead so that they are taught that to get to where they want to be, they have to do what the teacher requires. Behaviour Modification demands 1:1 interaction.

Some aspects of the curriculum clearly vary to the degree to which they can be introduced and sustained without 1:1 teaching. That is not to say, of course, that this is the most effective form of teaching, bearing in mind the caveats about the Jones and Meldrum research, but simply that it is difficult to conceive of any other approach. Music may be one these areas. Musical Interaction Therapy (Christie and Wimpory, 1986) involves a teacher or co-worker using improvised music to draw each individual child into a shared musical relationship or activity through which therapy may be pursued. A third party, providing the music, facilitates this interaction. Along similar lines, Movement Communication specialists work on a 1:1 basis with young autistic pupils by moving in unison with them, turn taking and mirroring their movements to produce a communicative intention (National Autistic Society, 1993).

In one Assessment Unit for 4–7 year old children in the West Country, the eight children who are normally in the Unit at any one time, for a period of 2–3 terms, have a variety of special educational needs. Out of any given group of these eight over the past three years, no more than one of the children has been diagnosed as having autism. Three children, whom I shall call Mark, Ned and Andrew, came to the Unit with an autistic diagnosis. Mark and Ned were said to be higher functioning Asperger, and Andrew was said to be autistic. All three children were totally different in the ways in which they presented themselves, in their level of functioning, in their behaviour and in the relationships they had with their parents and their professional entourage. Each child arrived at the Unit with varying degrees and types of information, despite the fact that all had been diagnosed.

Mark came to the Unit with his behaviours well documented. In particular, his parents had been highly significant in compiling Mark's detailed notes, which was potentially very helpful in knowing where to start with him. His parents made it clear that they welcomed a direct teaching strategy. A strategy evolved whereby for short periods during each day, he was given 1:1 teaching on specific skills. For example, Mark had very poor grip and had great difficulty in using both hands in a co-ordinated manner to carry out a task. Using scissors was a major problem for him, so the task of cutting along a straight line was broken down into small steps. By a process of backward chaining and 'hands on' physical guidance, Mark became able to complete the task unaided. The parents were shown this process and were able to work with him on a 1:1 basis at home, so reinforcing and developing the work in the Unit.

Ned came to the unit trailing clouds of destruction and disruption! He had previously been at a nursery where the atmosphere was so invigorating that he could not settle to any task. His home culture was similar to the nursery culture in so far as he was allowed freedoms which in a school setting could not be tolerated or managed. His major problem at the point of entry into the Unit was his anti-social behaviour, which not only hurt and frightened other children but also prevented any constructive learning taking place. The immediate task was to teach Ned alternative ways of communicating his anger, anxiety and frustration. He was a verbal child so needed to be taught appropriate responses in a variety of settings. The case was made for extra staffing so that his behaviour could be monitored and ameliorated as necessary. A classroom assistant was appointed, trained and worked, under the direction of the Teacher-in-charge of the Unit, on a 1:1 basis with Ned for 0.5 of the school day. The classroom assistant was also in the playground with him at playtime and lunch time because these were the times which Ned found most stressful. By intervening and giving him time out when he was showing signs of anxiety and offering him alternative ways of responding to the situation which had caused the distress, he slowly became less aggressive and threatening towards other children and adults. In the classroom, his work took place in a specially designated area, suitably demarcated so that he knew how much he had to do and in what sequence. The classroom assistant was in close proximity, supporting at all stages in the task.

Andrew, unlike Ned, had little language other than echolalic responses. Very little was known about Andrew when he came to the Unit so the first task was to gather information from his mother, a single parent. Contact with dad was rare for Andrew. A 0.5 classroom assistant support was immediately put in place with a facility for working with Andrew at playtime and lunch time. An assessment and intervention schedule was used (Aarons and Gittens, 1992b) to establish where a start could be made to work with Andrew. This schedule, produced by speech therapists, was normally administered on a 1:1 basis. Andrew used a specially constructed work booth to minimalize distractions and, unlike Ned, there was a greater element of seclusion. Having highlighted his strengths and weaknesses, the classroom assistant and teacher devised an intervention programme. Initially, this consisted of mainly interactive type activities ('round and round the garden'). These early activities led into visual perception skills work, for example, shape matching, simple construction tasks and naming of everyday objects. The 1:1 help enabled a choice to be made about the best time for Andrew to do these activities. When he finished what the Unit staff wanted him to do, he had access to a shelf of his own where he could choose to play with one of his favourite noisy toys.

At Sutherland House, Nottinghamshire, a specialist provision for children with autism, 1:1 teaching takes place by withdrawing individual children from a central playroom staffed by trained play therapists. Given the resources and a flexible working environment, this model is worth emulating. Even though only a small proportion of children in a school or Unit setting may be autistic, nonetheless, given that all children with special needs can benefit from quality 1:1 teaching, a stress on the possibility of using such time can be justified. In this sense, a teaching strategy particularly appropriate to pupils with autism would help all the pupils. Jones and Meldrum have not demonstrated that 1:1 teaching in itself will always be the most effective teaching strategy for working with pupils with autism but it would be difficult to compose intervention strategies for such children without drawing on 1:1. For thinking and learning skills, very special teaching strategies are needed (Jordan and Powell, 1990). Wendy Brown (1992) has drawn our attention to Kugler's claim that: 'a child with autism is more vulnerable than any other child of the same age' (Brown, 1992, p. 6).

For this reason alone, we need to ensure that the resource base is in place to allow this vulnerability to be minimized. Pupils with autism have rights to equal treatment as a minimum and deserve special discrimination in order to allow them to stand any chance of achieving fully functioning citizenship. Our attitudes and treatment towards those people who, through no fault of their own, find it difficult to become full members of society is one of the major criteria for judging the extent to which that society is civilized or barbaric. Our society, as far as autistic children is concerned, is generally intrigued by the presence of these strange children and can be sympathetic, to a point, with the difficulties parents have in controlling the behaviour of such children in public places. Autistic children stretch people's toleration towards different behaviour, stretch our intellectual ingenuity in getting at what these children think about and want from life, put pressure on the relationship between professional and lay authority, suggest we should resist a rampant form of universalism in curriculum and pedagogy and cry out for a transparently fair and efficient set of principles and policies for distributing educational resources.

REFERENCES

Aarrons, M. and Gittens, T. (1992b) *The Autistic Continuum. An Assessment and Intervention Schedule*. London: NFER Nelson.

Aarrons, M. and Gittens, T. (1992a) *The Handbook of Autism – A Guide for Parents & Professionals*. London: Routledge.

Allen, G. *et al.* (1987) *Community Education: An Agenda for Educational Reform*. Milton Keynes: Open University Press.

Andrews, C. (1992) 'Development of thought'. In Arendt, L. *Living and Working with Autism*. London: The National Autistic Society.

Baron-Cohen, S. (1987) 'Autism and symbolic play'. *British Journal of Developmental Psychology,* **5**, 139–48.

Bastiani, J. (1987) 'Professional versus lay authority'. In Allen, G. *et al. Community Education: An Agenda for Educational Reform*. Milton Keynes: Open University Press.

Brown, W. (1992) 'Positive Intervention'. In Module 2, Unit 4 of Autism Distance Learning Course. The University of Birmingham.

Brown, W. (1993) 'What is a good school for this child?' In Collection of Papers from Study Weekend on Asperger's Syndrome. London: Inge Wakehurst Trust.

Christie, P. and Hall, B. (1993) *Parents as Partners*. Autism Module of Autism Distance Learning Programme, University of Birmingham

Christie, P. and Wimpory, D. (1986) 'Recent research into the development of communicative competence and its implications for the teaching of autistic children'. *Communication*, **20**(1), 4–7.

Connelly, M. (1990) 'Foreword'. In Jordan, R. and Powell, S. *The Special Curricular Needs of Autistic Children: Learning and Thinking Skills*. London: The Association of Head Teachers of Autistic Children and Adults.

Daniels, H. and Ware, J. (1990) *Special Education Needs in the National Curriculum: The Impact of the E.R.A.*, The Bedford Way Series, University of London.

Dearing, R. (1993) In Jenkins, S. 'The Dearing Review'. *Devon Education News*.

Department of Education and Science (1978) *Special Educational Needs* (The Warnock Report). Report of the Committee of Enquiry into the Education of Handicapped Children and Young People. London: HMSO.

Department of Education and Science (1989) *Discipline in Schools* (The Elton Report). London: HMSO.

Frith, U. (1989) *Autism: Explaining the Enigma*. Oxford: Basil Blackwell.

Grandin, T. and Scariano, M. (1986) *Emergence Labelled Autistic*. Tunbridge Wells: Costello.

Jolliffe, T., Lansdown, R. and Robinson, R. (1992) *Autism: A Personal Account*. London: National Autism Society.

Jones, G. and Meldrum, E. (1993) *Preliminary Findings and Implications for Practice Arising from an Evaluative and Comparative Study of Current Interventions of Children with Autism*. London: Department of Health and Department for Education.

Jordan, R. (1990a) *The National Curriculum: Access for Pupils with Autism*. London: Inge Wakehurst Trust.

Jordan, R. (1990b) 'Personal and Social Education and the Pupil with Autism'. In Collection of Papers from Study Weekend. London: Inge Wakehurst Trust.

Jordan, R. and Powell, S. (1990) *The Special Curricular Needs of Autistic Children: Learning & Thinking Skills*. London: The Association of Head Teachers of Autistic Children & Adults.

Lewis, A. (1991) *Primary Special Needs and the National Curriculum*. London: Routledge.

Lovaas, O.I., Caloun, K. and Jada, J. (1989) 'The nature of behavioural treatment and research with young autistic persons'. In Gilberg, R. (ed.) *Diagnosis and Treatment of Autism*. New York: Plenum.

National Autistic Society (1993) *Approaches to Autism*. London.

NCC (1993a) *English in the National Curriculum*. York.

NCC (1993b) *Mathematics in the National Curriculum*. York.

NCC (1993c) *Modern Foreign Languages*. York.

OFSTED (1992) *Curriculum Organisation and Classroom Practice in Primary Schools*. London: HMSO.

Peacey, N. (1993) *Helping Children with Oral Communication Difficulties – A Team Approach*. Talk given at the College of St Mark and St John, Plymouth.

Schopler, E. and Mesibov, G.B. (eds) (1989) *Diagnosis and Assessment in Autism*. New York: Plenum.

Welch, M. (1988) *Holding Time*. London: Century Hutchinson.

Wing, L. (1988) 'The Continuum of Autistic Characteristics'. In Schopler, E. and Mesibov, G.B. (eds) *Diagnosis and Assessment in Autism*. New York: Plenum.

Wragg, E.C. (1989) *Primary Teachers and the National Curriculum*. Research Papers in Education. 4:3, 17–47.

Chapter 4

Children and Political Violence

INTRODUCTION

> The child's sob in the silence, curses deeper than the strong man in his wrath
> (Elizabeth B. Browning, from *The Cry of the Children*, quoted in Free the Children Alliance, 1987)

> Children of refugees, displaced persons, and migrants often have limited or no access to basic education and literacy programmes, but such programmes are crucial to their adaptation and survival. The lives of these children have been disrupted by war, famine, and/or civil conflict. Forced to acculturate to new worlds, often radically different from where they came, they require education to adjust to their new environment.
> (World Conference on Education for All, 1990)

The general focus which informed brief visits to South Africa and Mozambique in 1994 and 1995 was to examine ways in which educational policies and practices address significant social issues that condition and contextualize the education of children and their families. A special focus on the position of children in special circumstances, in particular children who have experienced political violence in one form or another, was chosen as an important aspect which demands a coherent response from educationalists. This chapter reports on the first stage of a long-term project concerned with the social condition of young people in special circumstances and focuses on what we know about the needs of children who have experienced political violence, and about the main features of significant intervention agencies and programmes.

The initial outcomes of the enquiry are shown in Figure 4.1. This illustrates the main academic and professional traditions which characterize analysis and work with children in special circumstances revealed by this initial review.

CHILDREN IN SPECIAL CIRCUMSTANCES IN MOZAMBIQUE: THE BACKGROUND

Mozambique gained its independence from Portuguese colonial rule in 1975 after a ten-

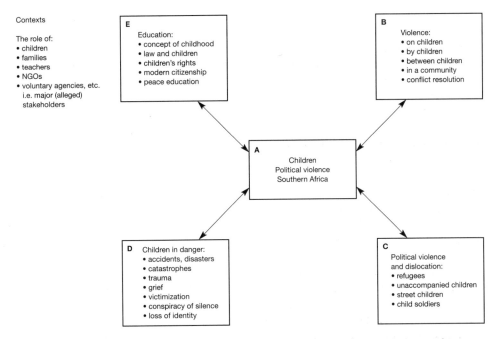

Figure 4.1 *Children and political violence, with special reference to Southern Africa – an overview of research and action approaches*

year armed struggle led by the national liberation movement, Frelimo. A one party state was established based on socialist development models. From 1975, the Mozambique National Resistance (MNR) or Renamo, with initial support from South Africa, fought to destabilize the Frelimo government until the cease-fire in October 1992. An estimated one million people died during the civil conflict (the total population in 1991 was 16 million), two million people were displaced and one and a half million people were forced to leave Mozambique for refuge in neighbouring countries (SCF, 1992). Mozambique suffers from multiple difficulties – the threat of continued civil conflict, regular droughts, floods and famines, a displaced population and a severe scarcity of skilled workers and foreign exchange. It is the world's poorest country, with a per capita income in 1992 of $76 (World Bank, 1992). The UK had a per capita income of $1500 in the same year.

A UNICEF (1989) report estimated that some quarter of a million children had either been orphaned or separated from their families. These children normally lack regular food and shelter, and might well be badly affected psychologically and physically by their experiences of political violence. Mozambique is generally a difficult country to be born in, to live in and to flourish in, as Table 4.1 indicates (SCF, 1992).

Table 4.1 *Child statistics, Mozambique, UK, 1992*

	Mozambique	UK
Population growth per year %	2.6%	0.2%
Infant mortality rate (0–1)	173/1000	8/1000
Child mortality rate (0–4)	297/1000	9/1000
Life expectancy at birth (years)	48	76

This brief sketch of the condition of children in Mozambique raises major questions about the morality of research and analysis of the situation of such children. I shall return to this theme but it needs to be established early in the chapter that there is no justification for conducting research which is directed towards the truthful description and analysis of human suffering unless the elimination of the suffering is the explicit aim of the research.

CHILDREN IN SPECIAL CIRCUMSTANCES IN SOUTH AFRICA: THE BACKGROUND

People throughout the world are liable to associate political violence during recent years with South Africa, but the causes, nature and distribution of the violence may not be so well known. The violence has involved populist insurrections against the former apartheid state, conflicts between supporters of the African National Congress (ANC) and Inkatha, and has been seen in local feuds or 'faction fights', sometimes involving the revival of the use of traditional 'cultural weapons' (du Toit, 1993). The prediction and fear that violence by blacks on whites would be widespread proved unfounded. Andre du Toit's superb paper offers a detailed historical analysis of what he calls the 'master-narrative' of the general project of modernization in South Africa.

In KwaZulu-Natal, endemic faction fights in certain rural areas took place, reflecting a strong legacy from the pre-modern period. The symbolic *assegais* and fighting sticks traditionally carried by Zulu men became a major feature of the violence. These weapons are not only efficient but suggest a long-standing struggle for freedom from oppression. The main social problems in KwaZulu-Natal stem from a set of interrelated developments such as land reclamation (demanded by dispossessed peoples), the demobilization and integration of former soldiers, including child soldiers and the return of people from forced exile: 'Mandlazini people won't see the New South Africa when they are still starving at Ntambanana' (ANC, 1993a). The Mandlazini people of north west Natal, for example, were moved from their traditional lands at Central Richards Bay to Ntambanana, some 60km inland, where there was no clean water, no employment, no plantation land and not enough appropriate land for cattle farming (ANC, 1993b).

A special feature of the conflict, which has apparently left a serious problem of widespread Post Traumatic Stress Disorder, was violence by the state against children. The ANC estimates that some 173,000 black South African children were held in detention during the 1970s and 1980s and of these, 120,000 were subject to violent treatment whilst detained (ANC, 1988). The UN Observer Mission in South Africa has deployed 60 civilian observers, in eleven regions, but especially in Witwatersrand-Vaal and KwaZulu-Natal, where most of the post-election violence has been recorded. From their

Table 4.2   *Child statistics, South Africa, UK, 1991*

	South Africa	UK
Population growth per year %	2.2%	0.1%
Infant mortality rate (0–1)	71/1000	9/1000
Child mortality rate (0–4)	95/1000	11/1000
Life expectancy at birth (years)	61	75

reports and the constant stream of press stories from South Africa, we learn that violence is still a popular method for resolving disputes. For many of these children in South Africa, structural violence is also a major aspect of their lives, as Table 4.2 illustrates.

Within this overall South Africa picture, there are wide variations between blacks, whites, coloureds and Asians. South Africa is the most unequal country in the world, where, for example, some 13 per cent of the population (white) own 80 per cent of the land (SCF, 1991).

FRAMEWORKS FOR ANALYSIS AND ACTION

Each of the four starting places shown in Figure 4.1 is not exclusive yet the review suggests that they are significantly different to justify putting into semi-watertight boxes in this way. Figure 4.1 shows that the analysis of children and political violence is both interdisciplinary and multi-disciplinary. Any analysis and any programme of intervention should be explicitly conscious of its own ideological and intellectual roots. Should the intervention programme claim to be driven by pragmatism or realism or some similar variant on the theme, then an analysis of the theory of human nature and social conditions which determines the pragmatism also needs to be explicit.

Understanding the consequences of political violence requires an understanding of the nature of the war or armed conflict, of the social, economic and political context (including causes) of the conflict, of the types of human rights violations carried out in the name of the conflict, the types of communities affected by the conflict and the nature of the individual, family and community resources available to survive, cope with and reconstruct after the conflict. These sorts of understandings are difficult to achieve, which in part explains why people who feel they have to act or intervene do so in the full knowledge that their understanding is often too limited to allow them to feel confident that intended outcomes will come about.

We know that programmes for children who have experienced armed conflict should be pro-people and people oriented, culturally appropriate, including gender sensitive, and participatory and democratic (Protacio-Marcelino, 1993). Political violence leads to claims for restitution, compensation and rehabilitation (Danieli, 1993a). The UN Convention on the Rights of the Child and the World Summit for Children have gone some way in setting out agreed minimum standards for children's survival, health and education and the minimum protection required by children against abuse, exploitation and neglect in war, at work or in the home (Munir, 1993). The focus of this paper will be on Box D in Figure 4.1, and work on the other elements in the model is part of the general project and will be reported in due course.

CHILDREN IN DANGER

On New Year's Eve, 1994, the *Guardian* newspaper carried a long article by Felicity Arbuthnot headed 'Iraq's innocents suffer the loss of childhood'. The article reports on a visit by Professor Magne Raundalen to Iraq with the International Harvard Study Team in order to inform UNICEF about the mental health of children in Iraq. According to

Professor Raundalen, these children are 'trapped within their trauma', and he and his colleagues have established Iraq's first trauma centre for children who have been affected by war.

Western newspapers have been very influential in telling the stories of children who have suffered from political violence. Naomi Richman's report on the *Psychological Effects of War on Children* (1988) was the first of a series of influential, widely publicized reports that she produced between 1988 and 1993. It described the experiences of children in Mozambique during the civil war and indicated the level and type of psychological damage caused to the affected children. In 1992, the *Psychologist Journal* devoted an entire edition to the current state of 'Psychological Research in Northern Ireland', which showed the extent and nature of psychologists' response to 'the troubles', including studies of children. In the USA, at Columbia University, New York, a major long-term research and action group, the Project on Children and War (POCAW) is an example of the many programmes of research and programme development projects set up to examine and respond to the condition of children during and after political violence. (See the 1993 report of Dr Mona Macksoud, the Director of Psycho-social research within POCAW, *Helping Children Cope with the Stresses of War*.) In South Africa, a notable feature of violence towards children arose from the policy of apartheid. Silove (1988), for example, claims that children were generally unable to comprehend why they had been put in jail. A 12-year-old black boy tells him: 'Life nowadays is like a sick butterfly. To many of us it is not worth living when it is like this.'

Legally, a child in South Africa is someone under the age of 17, and the experiences of some of these children under apartheid attracted worldwide attention. Influential reports include the 1986 study by the Lawyer's Committee for Human Rights (New York), *The War Against Children: South Africa's Youngest Victims*, and the ANC's Press statement on violence (1991) leading to the establishment of a Charter for Peace. The State of Emergency declared in South Africa in June 1986 was preceded by 'state violence against children of a scale without parallel in human history' (Majodina, 1989, p. 3). Majodina estimates that between 1984 and 1986, 11,000 children were detained without trial, 18,000 were arrested on charges arising from street protests and, overall, some 173,000 children experienced being held in police custody awaiting trial.

One of the most influential accounts of children in special circumstances comes from the United States Committee for Refugees (USCR). Established in 1958, as a public information and advocacy programme of the American Council for Nationalities Service, the USCR aims to 'encourage the American public to participate actively in efforts to assist the world's refugees'. Its report on *Children of Mozambique: The cost of Survival* (Boothby, 1988), arose from interviews with 504 children from 49 districts as part of a joint project between SCF and the Mozambique Directorate of Social Action. The focus of the study was on getting children's narrative accounts of their direct experience of war. These were children, aged between 6 and 15, who had lived in areas which became major battlefields. Boothby's study begins with a numerical survey of 'abuses and atrocities':

> Every child interviewed as part of this study had suffered from a range of traumatic and abusive experiences. More than three-fourths have witnessed killings. Almost 90% have seen people beaten or tortured. More than half have been forcefully separated from their families and used in a number of abusive ways; and about one in ten of those children abducted from their families have been forced to kill other human beings.   (Boothby, 1988, p. 4)

UNICEF in Maputo (Johnson and Martin, 1988) collected stories of brutalized children, children who had apparently been conditioned to kill: 'First they kill a pig or a goat as a group. Then they kill as an individual. Finally, they graduate to a human prisoner' (Captured Renamo child soldier). This boy soldier explains that the army, Frelimo, 'Won't shoot children, that children do as they are told and don't defect'. In 1987, UNICEF was claiming, based on government data, that a child was dying every four minutes as a result of political violence in Mozambique and Angola.

In Southern Croatia, Rumboldt and associates have done one of the rare longitudinal-studies of the physiological impact of war on children. They studied 6- to 7-year-old children from Split over a four-year period, two years before the war and during two years of the war. Children's growth rates were seen to be possibly affected, and affected to significantly different degrees, by the way in which the children responded to the atrocities, for example the degree of emotional stress experienced (Rumboldt *et al.*, 1994). In Kuwait, children who stayed during the 1990 Iraq occupation were reported as having multiple war-related exposures which led to over 70 per cent of the children in the study reporting moderate to severe post-traumatic stress reactions (Nader *et al.*, 1993). Studies of Arab children in Israel, the Gaza Strip and the West Bank include Elbedour (1993) and associates' account of adjustment levels, personality and psycho-pathology during a long-term conflict. Amongst several important UNICEF studies, reports on *Children in Especially Difficult Circumstances* (1990a) and *The Psycho-social Impact of Violence on Children in Central America* (1990b) include discussion of important general issues and the situation in the Americas. The work done by Calvo (1993) for UNICEF in the Philippines is a significant report not just because of its sensitive analysis of the situation of children in the Philippines but because of the emphasis on programme evaluation.

There are now a number of well-known established models for analysis and programme construction for children in special circumstances. The impact on the child of potentially traumatic circumstances appears to be determined by the age of the child or its developmental stage, the family situation or stage, the degree to which basic value systems have been formed and, maybe, dismantled and, generally, the change in psycho-biography. This is a typical psychological or psychotherapeutic approach. The direct experience of political violence from the different types of exposure to the situation of war will also be influential. Some children experience a direct life threat, or injury to themselves; they witness injury, even seeing grotesque death; they may see members of their family die or witness severe injury to loved ones, or hear cries for help to which they may be unable to respond (UNICEF, 1993a). The relationship of the child to the aggressor, as well as to the victim, could be significant.

The most general and popular psychological model asserts that a distorted life, for example, through exposure to political violence, leads to a distorted mind. This may not be inevitable. Children may well be able to deal with events through excluding or otherwise protecting themselves from trauma. For example, the degree to which a violent experience creates stress might be related to the child's state of readiness or anticipation. The number and sequence of experiences will also be important, where one single event may trigger a traumatic reaction to a series of experiences. The use of weapons and the type of weapons could be influential. A study of some 500 Israeli school age children's stress reaction to bombardment by SCUD missiles a month after the cease-fire showed, predictably, that proximity to sites where a SCUD had landed or knowledge of individuals hurt by the missiles was significant (Schwarzwald *et al.*, 1993).

Mona Macksoud (1993) offers a framework for parents and teachers to help them identify stress in young children. The approach relies on the child's account of a process, event or situation. Macksoud argues that stress, its incidence, level and type, will be related to the sorts of experiences the child has been exposed to, how they feel about these experiences, and which aspects of the experience the child perceives as most stressful and difficult to adjust to. Macksoud lists a range of 'typical' age-related reactions and goes on to explore the influence of home and school support and, generally, to discuss the creation for the child of a 'therapeutic' environment, a theme I shall return to. The political or socio-economic context, together with the nature of the conflict and the communities affected by it and the types and extent of human rights violations, will affect the ease and speed with which such a 'therapeutic environment' is achieved (Protacio-Marcelino, 1993).

The Red Cross (1993), in its *Guidelines for the Development of a Psychological Support Programme for Victims of Disasters and other Stressful Life Events*, emphasizes that we should treat children's trauma-related activities as normal reactions to abnormal events. This is an unpopular position with the psychotherapists since it denies the existence of a pathological response by the child, hence taking the analysis and treatment away from the otherwise monopolistic position of the mental health professionals. Most victims, the International Red Cross argues, 'do not need complex mental health interventions, but informed humanitarian support based on a knowledge of common human needs' (p. 5). This approach is echoed in Ager's (1993) work on the coping strategies found in Mozambican refugees. The framework here is to distinguish studies which are basically problem focused, emphasizing social circumstances from a person-centred approach, focusing on personal need and the means of adjusting to the difficulties. Ager also separates out responses or programmes which prioritize individual strategies from those concentrating on social or shared responses.

Post Traumatic Stress Disorder (PTSD) is the framework which dominates the psychological or psycho-therapeutic approach. Pynoos's (1985) *Post Traumatic Stress Disorders in Children* offers a comprehensive review of the literature. Things have moved on since 1985, however. It is now clear that a number of fallacies may be distorting the effective use of the PTSD construct (Raundalen *et al.*, 1990). These alleged fallacies are:

- Children are resilient and are infinitely capable of self-renewal.
- Adults who share the potentially traumatic experience are the best people to work with the child.
- Some experiences are too painful for the child to revisit and should be suppressed.

What then is a traumatic experience? Trauma often follows life threatening events, such as the experience of war, which have such a severe impact on the senses that the memory of the experience is strong, yet the personal inclination is to mobilize resistance to the experience. People who have been traumatized are frequently described as being in shock, or in a chronic state, with an expectation that the experience which triggered the trauma can be re-lived. Single Event Trauma (SET) should be distinguished from Extreme Situational Trauma (EST), according to Raundalen *et al.* (1990). Modern crisis psychology is perhaps the current dominant tool for analysis and treatment. The field has grown out of the work of psychologists attempting to find an understanding and then a treatment model which allows them to work for the recovery of victims of accidents, catastrophes and disasters, as well as the victims of violence. One major methodological problem in crisis psychology is to develop an impact of event or situation scale. This clearly has to be constructed out of the feelings of the victim, using psycho-biographical questions to evaluate the subjective exposure to a traumatic event or situation.

Working with children who have been victims or perpetrators of violence, of course, creates an additional layer of difficulty because there may well be a limited language capacity, similar in kind but not in cause to communication problems exhibited by autistic children. In some cases, children, like some traumatized adults, have stopped talking, may be in a deep and disturbing depression or may exhibit severe compulsive or obsessional behaviour. In such cases, the need for treatment is clear. However, it is possible that no 'outward' signs of personal damage are evident. Some agencies, such as UNICEF, to play safe, work from the assumption that certain types of experience will lead to damage in children, whether this is immediately obvious or not. For example, children who have had one or both parents killed, children who themselves have been physically injured by war, who have witnessed injury to others or caused injury to others (child soldiers), children who have been detained or punished because of their partici-pation in war or who have had to take major risks to their health because of war, are all deemed to be in need of support.

It is not clear, at this stage, whether there is a distinctly different sort of psycholog-ical response to war-time traumas, for example, occupation by a hostile enemy or violent political acts, such as bombings, and to peace-time traumas, such as accidents, cata-strophes, disasters, domestic violence, peer group violence or more generally, growing up in a violent community. Some children are simply abandoned or orphaned, may become isolated or dislocated and may be rounded up and put into some form of insti-tution which in itself may induce or deepen trauma (Mozambique National Directorate for Social Welfare, 1985 and 1987). Desjarlais (1993), in a Review Paper prepared for the Harvard Project on International Mental and Behavioural Health, quotes Richman, yet again, on children's brutality during the civil war in Mozambique and Nordstrom's revelations that children were involved in disembodiment. Whether violence is perpe-trated by children or on children, the standard psychologist's response is summarized by Dawes in Desjarlais (1993):

> In the absence of support, without some form of ideological belief structure and in the face of severe overwhelming stress such as torture, repeated harassment and witnessing the death or brutal treatment of those close to them, clinical disturbance may result.   (p. 56)

What we need to know are the determinants of different responses to traumatic events. The range of response varies in type and intensity, in frequency and complexity, and it is clear that some children, like some adults, cope. The main behavioural features induced by trauma are re-experience or re-enactment, suppression or avoidance, memory disturbance, physiological distress and exaggerated startle response (Raundalen *et al.*, 1990). We have seen that, if possible, we need to let children tell others about their harmful experience(s) and there are obvious parallels here in working with children who have been, or may have been, victims of sexual abuse. How do children communicate about stressful situations and events? James Garbarino and Frances M. Stott (1990), together with colleagues at the Erikson Institute, have explored the relationship between the contexts in which children talk to adults (home, school, day-care) and what they actually talk about. Their work may be useful for people working in the field of children and political violence. The first theme identified is that children communicate about their experiences in at least three ways:

- by answering direct questions
- by providing spontaneous reports about their lives
- using non-verbal messages, which may be the only possible form of communication for some children
  (The simplicity of this framework should be compared to the section in the previous chapter on communication and autistic children.)

'Talking cures' is a well-known proposition, and if events are sensitively and accurately reconstructed and assigned meaning, this may be the case. Of course, things can be made worse through intensifying the symptoms. The second theme which the Erikson Institute study reveals is that the philosophy of treatment is a determinant in how others will pursue the leads that the children offer. Three well known traditional role models for early childhood workers are described. The Erikson Institute identify what they call the 'maternal role' model which concentrates on keeping the children 'safe, comfortable, busy and happy' (Garbarino and Stott, p. 235). The 'therapeutic' model expects the worker to enable the child to reveal and understand their feelings and to work them through a mental health focus. The third model they call the 'instructional' model, which concentrates on the worker's selection and transfer of useful knowledge, such as 'coping skills'. The information offered by the child will have important consequences for the child's development and for the way in which this development is influenced by others. This takes us back to an earlier point about the morality of researching human suffering. When deciding whether to pursue information about an event or situation which is suspected to have contributed to trauma, we need to be clear that there is a clear possibility that the information can used constructively in the child's interest. Given this moral prescription, Garbarino argues that we have to generally act extremely sensitively when we elicit, interpret and evaluate the information we get from children, especially young children.

Principles for good practice in talking with children about sensitive issues are well established in the literature (Williamson, 1988), and could well be absorbed by professionals in other fields, such as those working with autistic children. Williamson is particularly concerned with providing guidelines for field workers who need to interview unaccompanied children and to prepare what he calls their 'social histories'. The dominant approach appears to begin with a narrative report of the incident or situation and the emotions and sensations experienced. The ease with which this account is forthcoming, the shape of the story, its detail, and so on, will vary enormously from child to child, both in terms of how the account comes to be told and what is actually said. Intensive interplay is usually advisable, not silent listening. The general consensus appears to be that the child should be carefully listened to and their feelings recognized and confirmed. Any responses, though, should follow the child, not predict or pre-empt. Turn taking may be appropriate, as may be the sharing of emotions. Principles such as these have in part come out of work with adults who were victims of the Holocaust. The work of the *Group Project for Holocaust*

Survivors and their Children, New York City, has been particularly influential (Danieli, 1993b).

Roper and Dawes (1992) collected 79 essays (in English) from more or less equal numbers of black and white South African children (mean age, almost 17 years). The essays were entitled 'My country, South Africa', and written in 1989. The opening statements by a black child and a white child are instructive and typical of the difference in perception found:

> The country I live in is South Africa. This country is ruled by tyrant rulers. What I mean is that the government of South Africa uses too much dictatorship. We as blacks are not allowed to participate at Parliament. We are only told what to do but we are not asked weather we like it or not. Our leadership is disorganised and will cause us to become thugs. We kill one another for the sake of money. For the sake of money we are promised to kill one another by the whites. We will be payed for that.   (Black child)

> South Africa is special. It has everything you want peace and quiet, and to be close to nature – go the Northern Transvaal ... You want beautiful beaches with warm seas – go to Durban ... You want excitement with shows and gambling – go to Sun City ... Even with all its problems of racialism and apartheid, South Africa is a wonderful place to live.   (White child)

In Northern Ireland, McWhirter *et al.* (1983) engaged in a rare example of a research project which actually attempted to reveal children's understanding of death, and violent death in particular. The study is rare because of a reluctance of researchers, or the parents, guardians or children, to discuss death. McWhirter talked to 200 children aged between almost 4 and almost 16 years of age, half living in the more peaceful part of Belfast and half not. Equal numbers of Protestant and Catholic children were in the study, and all of the children were given tests of verbal ability. The main finding of the study was that death by violence was not a salient dimension in the children's perception of death. Death was said to come from illness, especially cancer, from old age and from accidents, especially road traffic accidents. Between 1969 and 1979, out of a thousand deaths caused by the civil war, over half were in Belfast, over 70 per cent were civilians and of the thousand, almost 30 per cent died through the effects of explosions. The average number of deaths per year between 1979 and 1982 arising from the conflict was 100. The total population of Northern Ireland in the late 1970s was 1.5 million people and, of course, there was extensive media coverage of the violence. Also, the paraphernalia of violent death surrounded the children – the signs warning to be careful, the soldiers, the vehicle checkpoints, bag searching, frisking, wire grills, reduced slits in letter boxes and boarded up shops and houses.

McWhirter and colleagues offer a psychological, cognitive developmental model of the child's concept of death, suggesting that it is not until age 7–8 before children can offer an objective and physical explanation of death, and children are normally 10–12 years of age before the universality and inevitability of death is identified (McWhirter *et al.*, 1983). I did not come across any studies of children in Southern Africa which report directly on the child's concept and experience of death. McWhirter asked:

> What do you think happens to people when they die?
> Where do you think you go when you're dead?
> What do you think it would be like to be dead?
> [And most interestingly for the purposes of this review]
> What makes people die?   (p. 88)

McWhirter's interest was in examining the claim that 'Some writers ... have suggested that the most dramatic effects of traumatic events can be seen in the children of the affected areas and are evidenced in the meaning they attribute to those events' (p. 91). Of course, it may be that in Belfast, familiarity breeds contempt and the abnormal becomes normal (Dawes, 1990). On my first visit to Maputo, Mozambique, the shock of seeing so many amputee children on the streets soon wore off.

Workers with children who have been victims of political violence may well benefit from research done by or reported by the International Society for Traumatic Stress Studies (Danieli, 1993a). This Society regularly reports work on the 'conspiracy of silence' which can affect victim and worker alike. Neither 'knows where to begin' and a counter transference of guilt may be at the root of the silence. The victim cannot speak for fear of recognizing some part in causing or failing to prevent the violence and the worker takes on a collective, or social guilt for the event or situation. Rappaport talks about the 'trauma after the trauma' and Symonds discusses the 'Second Injury to Victims' (Danieli, 1993a).

The theme of counter transference is particularly interesting and is a specific theme within the general issue of the morality of relatively well-off researchers and interventionists working on or with people considerably worse off than themselves. A simple, but vivid reminder of the issue faced me when taking photographs of poor children in Mozambique and KwaZulu-Natal and when drinking tea in Belfast, Northern Ireland with the elderly victims of sectarian directed crimes of breaking and entering. Counter transference themes include:

• The bystander's guilt (happy, protected, childhood).
• The possibility of exploitation because of a failure of nerve – a reluctance to turn down requests for help which may arise even where such requests stand no chance of being met.
• The objectification of human suffering, which is an extreme reaction by the researcher or therapist to the problem of being 'sucked in'.
• Anger or rage towards the victim, because, say, of a belief in the victim's acquiescence to violence (perhaps common amongst male researchers investigating the physical abuse of women by men in domestic settings?).
• Sharing the nightmare, for example where the victim's grief through witnessing or experiencing the death or damage to loved ones becomes part of the other person's psychological being.
• The loss of innocence, on both sides, because of the story of humiliating or barbaric behaviour.

A general research problem here is best described as the problem of privileged voyeurism, where the intervention is extended beyond reasonable limits. 'Investigatory journalists', such as John Pilger, have often been subject to this critique and certainly newspaper stories of atrocities carried out by children during the civil war in Mozambique may, in part, have come from discussions with children who were encouraged to reveal such stories (Boothby *et al.*, 1988).

Until the October elections in Mozambique, the ruling Frelimo government was analysing the problem of children in difficult circumstances in the context of putting resources into implementing a national–regional–local delivery system. The Secretary of

State for Social Action, together with Provincial Departments for Social Action, both handed down and received suggestions for policy and practice from Local Commissions for Children in Special Circumstances, and the daily implementation of policy was in the hands of People's Democratic Organizations, usually also supported by non-governmental organizations (NGOs). One seemingly successful policy for displaced or orphaned children was to find substitute families for them which worked well, it is claimed, because of the strong familial obligations felt by Mozambican substitute families towards children other than their own (Charnley and Langa, 1992). Children are placed in substitute families after family tracing programmes fail to reveal the whereabouts of the child's parents or find that the parents are dead (Bonnerjea, 1994). Such children are frequently characterized, before placement with a family, as 'refugee children'. Some countries keep the term 'refugee children' as their general categorization within which to place children who have been victims of political violence, but it is clear that children can also become refugees because of natural disasters, such as famine or flood. Children who have suffered political violence may become a sub-set within the refugee category (Ressler *et al.*, 1988). The title of Ressler's useful book, *Unaccompanied Children. Care and Protection in Wars, Natural Disasters and Refugee Movements*, suggests the range of categories and sub-categories used. The book itself offers sections on different countries' experiences of unaccompanied children and on psychological approaches to working with such children, and usefully reviews the law, human rights and children and a variety of treatment programmes.

The stress on the family, its presence or absence, and the experience of members of the family, if present, of political violence, as the focus of attention for the welfare of the child in difficult or special circumstances, is at the heart of many intervention programmes (Williamson and Moser, 1987). This is seen in such programmes as clearly preferable to the institutional care which refugee camps or orphanages can offer. In Pietermaritzburg, KwaZulu-Natal, I was told of a hospital which housed more than three hundred children who had been victims of political violence, had no other place to go and were allowed to live in the hospital. The children were known and named by either the place where they were found or by the ward or other area of the hospital they lived in. Save the Children Fund, for example, supports extensive family tracing studies in Mozambique and elsewhere because of its commitment to establishing some sort of family life for children in special circumstances (SCF, undated; Miller, 1990; see also Boothby, 1989).

Family-oriented programmes exist within a broader decision making framework of intervention for children in special circumstances. Calvo (1993), in a report specifically concerned with the Philippines, attempts to evaluate community-based psycho-social therapy programmes for children who have experienced what he calls 'armed conflict'. Calvo's report, to UNICEF, distinguishes 'area-based' approaches, which are 'in house' (an unfortunate phrase), offered by local providers, from 'module-based', which are controlled by outsiders. His conclusion is that a mix is needed. Protacio-Marcelino (1993) suggests that types of programme can be distinguished by their particular conceptual and centre–local configuration, by the type of service offered (direct–curative, indirect–preventative), and by the specific types of interventions. For example, some programmes stress an individual, clinical approach; others a group approach, using play, peer group and family – if present; whilst others focus on the use of indigenous therapies, such as faith healing, pranic healing and traditional medicines.

A major NGO, Redd Barna, in Mozambique, in its work with child soldiers, has carried out a rehabilitation programme which attempts to reunite former child soldiers with their family or with their locality (Jareg, 1993). Danieli (1985), whose work on the Holocaust survivors and their children has already been highlighted, has examined the 'intergenerational transmission of victimisation'. This leads him to a categorization of families, as follows:

- 'Fighter families' – these build, achieve, remain independent and seem to engage in compulsive activity.
- 'Numb families' – these are silent, invisible, play down emotions and suggest cautious pessimism.
- Families of 'those who made it' – a less homogeneous group, they demand commemoration, live in the past and deny its effects on their present.
- 'Victim families' – depressed, worried, have a fear of the outside world, full of mistrust; members symbiotically cling to the family and the family itself is a closed system.

I know of no similar attempt to categorize family responses to the trauma experienced by children who are victims of political violence. Many studies, however, according to Kanji (1990, p. 101):

> suggest that the gravity of the effects of war-related experiences on children depend fundamentally on factors linked to family and community conditions and responses. The loss of close relatives and other 'significant persons' has been found to be particularly traumatic, especially for younger children. The approach to assisting children will be affected by the importance attached to the role of the family and community in alleviating the effects of traumatic experiences on children.

We have to look to a study of school age children in the former Yugoslavia for the strongest statement found on what sort of general programme of reconstruction should be in place for child victims of political violence:

> Children's conceptualisation and understanding of the world, including moral development, development of empathy and of tolerance and democratic values, is severely jeopardised in times of war. For this reason, a specific programme for development of toleration, empathy and co-operation abilities in children should form the base for restructuring their confidence in the world and the future.   (Stuvland, 1993, p. 4)

What sort of programme might this be? The strength of the Kanji (1990) article is that intervention programmes are reviewed by her within a critical development studies framework. She identifies a 'Residual Approach', directed at the child particularly at risk from trauma, and a 'Community-centred Approach', where although the needs of vulnerable children are targeted, the programmes focus more generally on the needs of the families and communities of which they are a part. The first of these she is unhappy with because it smacks of short-termism, emergency led, leaving the individual (family?) to sort things out for the long term, 'through individual effort in the market place' (p. 103). The second, which she also characterizes as a 'Basic needs approach to development', is criticized for an over-reliance on the state, since the state may lack the infrastructure needed to implement broad development policies:

> There is a world of difference between establishing policies and executing them with national funds, and having to resell them to a plethora of different agencies with different

philosophies, methods and constraints. The time spent by government officials, responsible for planning and supporting programmes at national and provincial levels, responding to the different requirements of each agency constitutes a severe waste of scarce resources.

(p. 104)

The third approach, the 'Selective Approach', associated with UNICEF in particular, stresses 'selective interventions targeted at children' and, according to Kanji, 'fits well with economic adjustment policies implemented in so many underdeveloped countries in the 1980s' (p. 104). UNICEF has certainly rethought its approach and now implements policies which attempt to both target the psycho-social problems children experience, together with trying to negotiate a peace for children, even promoting the concept of 'children as zones of peace', where children are seen as a 'neutral, conflict-free zone in human relations' (UNICEF, 1987, p. 41), and to do all of this within a conscious policy of transition from conflict to development (UNICEF, 1992). Such an approach still needs to arise from an awareness of the sorts of detailed research studies which stress the nature of the individual response to violence. For example, Chimienti and Abu Nasr's (1992) study in Lebanon examines the mental health of children living during war. They differentiate the children by age (3–9) and gender, and focus on how the age and gender of the child interacts with the mother's reaction to stress. In Mozambique, McCallin and Fozzard (1990) also focused on the relationship between mothers and children who have become refugees as a result of the conflict.

EDUCATION, POLITICAL VIOLENCE AND CHILDREN

In the Sudan, the UN estimate that some 20,000 children have been separated from their families. Gregory Barrow, reporting from the Southern Sudan, reports on UNICEF's repatriation programme which has traced parents and relocated them to villages away from the fighting. The children, largely boys, were given 'repatriation' kits to help them to adapt: blankets, mosquito nets, sewing kits, and pencil and paper for them to catch up with their education, 'Sudanese children attach great importance to schooling. UNICEF has been training the few remaining teachers in Sudan to help the boys' (*Guardian*, 5 January, 1995). This fits with one of the main thrusts of UNICEF's work which is to examine and implement the specific contribution which teachers can make to promoting the welfare of children who have suffered from political violence. For example, it appears that their guide, *Helping Children Cope with the Stresses of War: A Manual for Trainers of Trainers* (1993a), is indicative of the sorts of practical guides which UNICEF are increasingly turning to. This suggests some growth in confidence of our knowledge of trauma and children since, any publication of a 'manual' endorsed by UNICEF legitimates the approach advocated for some governments and agencies as the current orthodoxy. UNICEF organized a two day training workshop concerned with 'Children in Armed Conflict'. (1993) which included outline proposals for a curriculum on education for peace, an approach which accords with Stuvland's views quoted above and a theme I shall return to.

The approach of the International Red Cross has also been mentioned, stressing, as it does, 'informed humanitarian support' rather than 'complex mental health interventions' (1993). Nonetheless, the IRC offers a training programme which enables workers to integrate basic psychological support into any intervention scheme. Their training includes the following formal courses (module titles): psychological first aid; personal awareness; volunteers working in the community; a management module; training for professional, especially mental health professionals; and specialist modules, such as 'stress in the workplace' and 'HIV/AIDS'. We have also seen that workers with victims can experience psychological damage themselves and there are now an increasing number of descriptions of programmes which attempt to address this issue. Sterns (1993) offers a useful review of these training courses. Equipping workers to work in specific locations is exemplified in the work described by Veale (1993) in her report on the training of street educators and youth workers in Ethiopia.

In Durban, KwaZulu-Natal, the Olive Information Service has examined the role of training, education and research in supporting both affirmative action programmes, which they characterize as ideologically driven by a belief in redress, and in capacity-building programmes, seen as 'neutral'. This work is described by Dolan and de Beer (1994), who were concerned with evaluating programmes designed to promote the research skills of black activists. Also in Durban, in the Pinetown area, the Pinetown-Highway Child and Family Welfare Society employs 26 social workers, employed by SCF and paid for by specific Comic Relief revenue, to work with children who have suffered child abuse, detention or general neglect. The approach stresses recreational activities, advice and information services and, where appropriate, seeks foster homes for the children rather than institutional care (SCF, 1991). This was the only mention made of social workers in any of the sources cited in this chapter.

The role of NGOs in Southern Africa has been the subject of much debate though no definitive review and recommendations for the role of NGOs in responding to the condition of children who are or have experienced political violence was found. The most interesting account of NGOs in Southern Africa, an account which has significant implications for NGOs working with children in special circumstances, is that of Jenny Rossiter and Robin Palmer (1990). They suggest that NGOs require a paradigm shift which they are reluctant to engage in. The shift is dramatically represented through presenting lists of the current favourite and least-favourite words in NGO development vocabulary.

Table 4.3 below is taken from Rossiter and Palmer's analysis, and they talk of a 'religious' attachment to the favourite position.

These approaches should not be exclusive. Even though Rossiter and Palmer attack NGOs for clinging to the favourite ideology and being reluctant to shift to the less

Table 4.3   *Favourite and least-favourite NGO words*

Favourite	Least-favourite
empowerment, partnership	product, economic analysis
process, animation	growth, cost effective
participation, grassroots	efficiency, accountability
additionality, networking	decisions, hierarchies
strategizing, brainstorming	material benefits
workshops, programming	effective management
evaluation, training	enterprise
gender awareness, non-project work	
the poorest of the poor	
working groups/parties	
task forces	
resourcing/flagging up	
pre-identification missions	

favoured position, there is clearly no necessary contradiction since, crudely, approaches are needed which are simultaneously democratic and efficient.

The UNCHR claim that 'Education is a human right. The education of refugees as any other need is the responsibility of the government in the country of asylum' is taken as the bottom line by the World University Service (WUS) in its Refugees Education Charter (WUS, 1990). More specifically, we need to think about the role which the school can play in promoting the welfare of children and communities who are 'under Fire' (Schwartz, 1982). Schwartz was particularly concerned to examine the role of the school in Northern Ireland during a period of conflict but also visited the South Bronx area of New York (violent crime), Israel and Boston (violent struggle around school desegregation). Simple yet powerful questions were asked of teachers:

> What were the effects on the children of the violence around them? How did the effects manifest themselves in the classroom? What was the impact of the violence on teachers and schools? What were teachers and schools doing to cope? (Schwartz, 1982, p. 44)

Schwartz found that children's respect for the law and authority were said to have deteriorated, that codes of behaviour had become debased and that there was a general lack of respect for the fabric of the schools. A university professor is quoted as suggesting: 'I wonder whether we should be so subject-centred in our teacher training colleges and not more child-centred' (p. 45). This is not a conclusion that is particularly tied to an analysis of the study of children and political violence. Nonetheless, it does raise the spectre of the school as a sanctuary from life, a metaphor with a long, powerful history. It took the greatest of twentieth century educational philosophers, John Dewey, to attack that position. Schools, he argued (1956), should offer a genuine form of active community life, instead of a place set apart in which to learn the lessons.

Dewey's position implies that schools should not ignore significant aspects of social life which affect the welfare of children and their families. How, then, might schools in Mozambique, South Africa and Britain respond to the phenomenon of children in special circumstances because of some experience of political violence? At this stage in the project, I want only to suggest that the subject of violence itself needs clarification. I shall conclude by offering some first thoughts on the experience of political violence and then outline some of the main themes which have emerged from this first stage of the inquiry.

THE CONCEPT OF POLITICAL VIOLENCE

There have been many attempts to categorize the various types of political violence (Desjarlais, 1993, offers a valuable review). We know that children can be victims of political violence, either as perpetuators or recipients. For example, in Pietermaritzburg, KwaZulu-Natal, I spoke to children who were living in a social situation where 90 per cent of all violence (which includes political violence) is carried out by young people and where, during the 1984–86 period, assault was the largest single cause of adolescent mortality for 10- to 14-year-old black South African children (Desjarlais, 1993). We need to understand the specific use of the concept of violence as used in the term, 'children and political violence', and to clarify what we need to do in order to 'understand' this violence (du Toit, 1993). Violence involves the use of force which leads to physical or mental injury to people and may also involve more general violations of human rights and dignities:

> Political violence is typically differentiated from other forms of violence by claims to a
> special moral or public legitimation for the injury and harm done to others, as by the repre-
> sentative character of the agents and targets of these acts of violence. (du Toit, 1993, p. 3)

In Mozambique, South Africa and Northern Ireland, certain kinds of political
violence have taken on a special significance extending far beyond the actual harm
caused. In Mozambique, interest has focused on children's use of violence against
other children, on children as child soldiers. In South Africa, most attention has been
paid to violence by the state towards children, where children have been at the front
line of resistance to a prevailing political regime and have been countered with force.
In Northern Ireland, the stress has been on seeing how far children have managed
to live 'normal' lives, have not associated themselves with violence or have disasso-
ciated themselves from the civil war. The mix of political violence and children is a
particularly problematic one. There is some degree of presumption, at least, that the
two should not mix – that children should not be combatants, that they deserve
special treatment from the state when suspected of crimes against the state, and that
they deserve a 'normal' upbringing, sheltered from any kind of violence.

CONCLUSION

This review was stimulated by current involvement in an educational reconstruction
project in Mozambique, by visits to Mozambique and KwaZulu-Natal in October, 1995
and by previous involvement in Britain in a peace education project which involved a
visit to Belfast, Northern Ireland, in the Spring of 1979. The general aim of the project,
as shown in Figure 4.1, is to understand the phenomenon of children and political
violence, and to suggest what sort of educational responses appear to be worthwhile.
This first part of the project has focused on the identification of studies that reveal data
and examples of political violence which involve young people, and on finding significant studies of children and political violence, particularly in Mozambique and, to a
lesser extent, in South Africa and Northern Ireland. The following themes suggest
further work arising from this first stage, themes which will alter the specific focus,
though not the general approach suggested by the overall framework:

1. The role of social research in the investigation of topics where there is the clear possibility of unanimity in condemning and seeking the elimination of problem (see
   Jablensky *et al.*, 1991, on 'Ethical Issues in Refugee Care and Provision') – that is,
   political violence.
2. The role of social research in the promotion of solutions to complex phenomena
   (where interventions, for example by teachers or care workers, are vital but generally ill informed, even misinformed) in vital areas of human welfare such as the
   elimination of suffering through trauma (the ethics of uncertainty in social research).
3. Explaining the lack of reference in the studies in Southern Africa and Northern
   Ireland of children and political violence and trauma, to what might be similar fields
   of enquiry – that is, child abuse and sexual abuse of children and trauma induced by
   political violence in any country.
4. Given the focus on families as the context for the recovery of damaged children and
   the emphasis on communication problems in children caused by trauma, why there is
   apparently little work done on or by social workers and speech and language thera-

pists in the area. Studies of the communication problems facing children with autism, for example, could be of interest to people working with war-traumatized children.

5. More generally, the studies of these children and the programmes in place to help them are seldom seen to break out of a narrow focus and ask whether approaches to working with children with similar problems or symptoms, albeit with different causes, could be useful (Allen and Martin, 1992).

6. The sources for information about children and political violence in Mozambique and South Africa are few. In Mozambique, a few commentators have dominated the narrative about child soldiers or children being violent towards other children. There appear to be different camps here, one of which believes that the reports that have dominated the literature have led to an exaggeration of incidents and a dramatization of children's accounts of political violence. In South Africa, the flow of information is dominated by the ANC and focuses on child state detainees, yet we know that the ANC itself is not free of crimes of torture, ill-treatment and execution (Amnesty International, 1992). In Northern Ireland, the research into children and political violence appears to have been totally dominated by psychologists, and although valuable (see, for example, Fields, 1975) it reflects little interest in social context.

Low intensity conflicts in impoverished countries have become the most frequent form of large scale conflict in the world. By 'low intensity' is meant 'total war at grassroots level' (Desjarlais, 1993). This type of war is characterized by control over a population, not a territory, through destruction and terrorism and where brutality against civilians, as in South Africa in the use of 'cultural' weapons by Inkatha, is governed by what Santiago has called 'an aesthetics of terror' (Desjarlais, 1993). Life then can only be lived at a continued and fearful intensity. The contribution which children make to the perseverance of this state by being perpetrators or recipients of political violence and the impact on children as possible bystanders, continues to call for a creative and committed response from the research community and from formal, informal and non-formal education programmes.

REFERENCES

African National Congress (1988) *In-house seminar*. July, Johannesburg.
African National Congress (1991) *Press statement on violence*. 27 April, Johannesburg.
African National Congress (1993a) *Negotiations Bulletin, No. 32*. 8 July, Johannesburg.
African National Congress (1993b) *National Land Commission, Land Update*, Johannesburg.
Ager, L. (1993) *Psychological Coping Strategies in Mozambican Refugees*. Paper to the III European Congress on Psychology, Tampere, Finland.
Allen, G. and Martin, I. (eds) (1992) *Education and Community: The Politics of Practice*. London: Cassell.
Amnesty International (1992) *Torture, Ill-treatment and Executions in ANC Camps*. Johannesburg, December.
Arbuthnot, F. (1994) 'Iraq's innocents suffer the loss of childhood'. *Guardian*, 31 December.
Bonnerjea, L. (1994) *Family Training: A Good Practice Guide*. London: SCF.
Boothby, N. (1989) *Helping Traumatised Children: A Training Manual for a Treatment and Family Unification Program*. Maputo: SCF.
Boothby, N. *et al.* (1988) *Children of Mozambique: The cost of Survival*. New York: USCR.
Calvo, L. (1993) *Overview of the Evaluation of Community Based Psycho Social Therapy Programmes for Children in Situations of Armed Conflict*. New York: UNICEF.

Charnley, H. and Langa, J. (1992) *Social Welfare Interventions for Unaccompanied Children in Mozambique*. Maputo: SCF.

Chimienti, G. and Abu Nasr, J. (1992) 'Children's reactions to war-related stress II'. *International Journal of Mental Health,* **21**(4) (Winter 92/93), 72–86.

Curran, P. (1988) 'Psychiatric aspects of terrorist violence. Northern Ireland, 1969–1987'. *British Journal of Psychiatry*, **153** (October), 470–5.

Danieli, Y. (1985) 'The treatment and prevention of long term effects and intergenerational transmissions of victimisation'. In Figley, C.R. *Trauma and Its Wake*. New York: Brunner-Mazel.

Danieli, Y. (1993a) In Williams, M.B. and Somer, W. *Handbook of Post Traumatic Therapy*. New York: Praeger.

Danieli, Y. (1993b) *Group Project for Holocaust Survivors and Their Children*. New York: UNICEF.

Dawes, A. (1990) 'The effects of political violence on children'. *International Journal of Psychiatry*, **25**, 13–31.

Desjarlais, R. (1993) *Political Violence and Mental Health*. A Review Paper prepared for the Harvard Project on International Mental and Behavioural Health. Cambridge, MA: Harvard University Press.

Dewey, J. (1956) *The School and Society*. Chicago: University of Chicago Press.

Dolan, C. and de Beer, M. (1994) *From Problems to Solutions*. Discussion document, ANC Education Workshop, Johannesburg, July.

du Toit, A. (1993) *Understanding South African Political Violence: a New Problematic?* New York: United Nations Research Institute for Social Development.

Elbedour, S. *et al.* (1993) 'Children at risk: psychological coping with war and conflict in the Middle East'. *International Journal of Mental Health*, **2**(3) (Fall), 33–52.

Fields, R. (1975) 'Psychological genocide: the children of Northern Ireland'. *Journal of Psycho-History*, **3**(2), 201–24.

Free the Children Alliance (1987) *Children and Detention*. Johannesburg.

Garbarino, J. and Stott, F. M. (1990) *What Children Can Tell Us*. New York: Jossey Bass.

Jablensky, M.D. *et al.* (1991) *Stress Research Reports No. 229*. The First International Conference on the Mental Health and Well-being of the World's Refugees and Displaced Persons. Stockholm, Sweden.

Jareg, E. (1993) *Rehabilitation of Child Soldiers in Mozambique*. Maputo: Redd Barna.

Johnson, P. and Martin, D. (1988) *Victims of Apartheid: Refugees, Returnees and Displaced Persons in Southern Africa*. Paper presented at the Oslo Conference on the Plight of Refugees, Returnees and Displaced Persons in Southern Africa.

Kanji. N. (1990) 'War and children in Mozambique: Is international aid strengthening or eroding community-based policies?' *Community Development Journal*, **25**(2), 102–12.

Lawyer's Committee for Human Rights (1986) *The War Against Children: South Africa's Youngest Victims*. December. Washington.

Macksoud, M. (1993) *Helping Children Cope with the Stresses of War*. New York: UNICEF.

Majodina, Z. (1989) *Factors Affecting Coping Modes Among South African Exiled Children*. Paper presented to the International Congress on Civil Rights, 16–18 June, Haikko, Finland.

McCallin, M. and Fozzard, S. (1990) *Impact of Traumatic Events on the Psychological Well-being of Mozambican Refugee Women and Children*. Maputo: International Catholic Child Bureau.

McWhirter, C. *et al.* (1983) 'Belfast children's awareness of violent death'. *British Journal of Social Psychology*, **22**(11), 81–92.

Miller, C. (1990) *Mozambique Family Tracing and Unification Programme*. London: SCF.

Mozambique National Directorate for Social Welfare (1985) *National Seminar on Children in Difficult Circumstances*. Maputo: Mozambique Ministry of Health.

Mozambique National Directorate for Social Welfare (1987) *Programme in Support of Children in Difficult Circumstances, 1985–1986*. Maputo: Mozambique Ministry of Health.

Munir, A.B.B. (1993) 'Child protection: principles and applications'. *Child Abuse Review*, **2**(2) (June), 119–26.

Nader, K.O. *et al.* (1993) 'A preliminary study of Post Traumatic Stress Disorder and grief among the children of Kuwait following the Gulf Crisis'. *British Journal of Clinical Psychology*, **32**(4) (November), 407–16.

Protacio-Marcelino, E. (1993) *Types of Psycho Social Programmes for Children in Armed Conflict*. New York: UNICEF

Psychologist Journal (1992) *Psychological Research in Northern Ireland* (special issue).

Pynoos, R.S. (ed.) (1985) *Post Traumatic Stress Disorders in Children*. London: SCF.

Raundalen, M. *et al.* (1990) *Reaching the Children Through the Teachers. Helping the War Traumatised Child. A manual*. Geneva: International Red Cross.

Red Cross (1993) *Guidelines for the Development of a Psychological Support Programme for Victims of Disasters and Other Stressful Life Events*. Geneva: International Red Cross.

Ressler, E. *et al.* (1988) *Unaccompanied Children. Care and Protection in Wars, Natural Disasters and Refugee Movements*. Oxford: Oxford University Press.

Ressler, E. *et al.* (1993) *Children in War. A Guide to the Provision of Services*. Geneva: UNICEF.

Richman, N. (1988) *Psychological Effects of War on Children*. London: SCF.

Richman, N (1991) *Reconciliation, Revenge? The Legacies of War*. London: SCF.

Richman, N. (1992) *Helping Children in Difficult Circumstances*. London: SCF.

Richman, N. (1993) 'Annotation: Children in situations of political violence'. *Child Psychology and Psychiatry*, **34**(8), 1286–302.

Roper, K. and Dawes, A. (1992) *The Use of Discourse Analysis in the Study of Children's Perceptions of South Africa*. Conference paper, Dept of Psychology, University of Cape Town.

Rossiter, J. and Palmer, R. (1990) *Northern NGOs in Southern Africa: Some Heretical Thoughts*. Paper presented to the University of Edinburgh, Centre of African Studies, Conference on Critical choices for the NGO community.

Rumboldt, M. *et al.* (1994) 'The impact of war upon the pupil's growth in Southern Croatia'. *Child Care, Health and Development*, **20**(3), 189–96.

SCF (undated) *Children in Difficult Circumstances*. London.

SCF (1992) *Country Report, South Africa*. London.

SCF (1993) *Country Report, Mozambique*. London.

Schwartz, R.E. (1982) 'Children under fire: the role of the schools'. *American Journal of Orthopsychiatry*, **53**(3), 409–19.

Schwarzwald, J. *et al.* (1993) 'Stress reaction of school-age children to the bombardment by SCUD missiles'. *Journal of Abnormal Psychology*, **102**(3), 404–10.

Silove, D.M. (1988) 'Children of apartheid: a generation at risk'. *The Medical Journal of Australia*, **148**, 346–53.

Sterns, S. (1993) 'Psychological Distress and Relief Work: Who helps the helpers?' *Refugee Participation Network*, **15**, 328.

Stuvland, R. (1993) *School Age Children Affected by War: The UNICEF Program in Former Yugoslavia*. New York: UNICEF.

UNICEF (1987) *Children on the Front-line*. New York.

UNICEF (1988) *The Situation of Children and Women in Mozambique*. New York.

UNICEF (1990a) *Children in Especially Difficult Circumstances*. New York.

UNICEF (1990b) *The Psycho Social Impact of Violence on Children in Central America*. New York.

UNICEF (1992) *Rehabilitation of Children in Armed Conflict*. New York.

UNICEF (1993a) *Helping Children Cope with the Stresses of War. A Manual for Trainers of Trainers*. New York.

UNICEF (1993b) *Childhood Trauma: Understanding and Treatment*. New York.

Veale, A. (1993) *Training Street Educators and Youth Workers*. Refugee Programme Centre, Oxford (unpublished).

Williamson, J. and Moser, A. (1987) *Unaccompanied Children in Emergencies*. Geneva: International Social Service.

Williamson, J. (1988) *Guidelines for Interviewing Unaccompanied Minors and Preparing Social Histories*. New York: UNCHR.

World Bank (1992) *Annual Report*. New York.

World Conference on Education for All (1990) *Meeting Basic Learning Needs: Vision for the 1990s*. Background document. Jomtien.

World University Service (1990) *Refugee Education Policy for the 1990s: Towards Implementing the Refugee Education Charter*. London: Education and Training Working Group.

Part III

Managing Uncertainty in Higher Education

Chapter 5

Assessment in Higher Education: Stress, Strain and Coping

INTRODUCTION

The assessment of students' work is one of the core activities of academic staff in higher education. Putting a value on other people's efforts is often so significant to those who do the valuing and those who receive the valuation that this activity must be taken extremely seriously by all parties. It is because of the importance of getting the value or grade right that this academic activity seems, on the surface, to be one aspect of academic work that can be stressful and lead to strain for academic staff. Even where grades are assigned by computer reading of student-completed standardized assessment tasks, at some point staff are likely to be in contact with students who have received disappointing grades. Moreover, it is not always easy to be totally confident that the correct grade has been awarded. One of the clear outcomes of the tragic suicides of students at British universities in recent years – suicides which are generally reported in the press as being to do with 'pressure' that is, with the pressure to conform socially and/or to perform according to self, parent, former teacher at school, friends' or faculty expectations – has been an increased need and willingness of staff to discuss and expose their anxieties about the possible impact of a grade on the student concerned. Some faculty have sought refuge in the system whereby an external examiner has the ultimate responsibility for the grade awarded. Any 'problematic' cases are devolved forthwith to the luckless (underpaid) external. The first point, then, is that it is possible to examine the process of assessing students' work in HE as a high risk activity. This then contributes to our understanding of stress and strain among academic staff and to the study of occupational stress in general.

When a grade is assigned to a piece of work submitted by a candidate for an award in a British university, what sort of decision is this? We know that this decision involves assigning one grade rather than any other – the valuation can never be equivocal within the grading system used. Both exam boards and students want a mark. We have highly developed and ritualized systems for arriving at agreed marks, systems which are designed, in part, to deal with differences of view which may emerge concerning the value of a piece of assessed work, or an overall valuation of the student. Economists are interested in value and decisions about value so my second point is to suggest that economic analysis might offer some insights into the decision to assign one value, a grade, rather than any other.

It would be interesting to explore the decision-making strategies which academic staff claim influence the process of assigning a value to the student's work and, thereby, also assigning, in the student's perception, a value to them as a person. For in so far as we have now a raised political consciousness of the self, assigning a grade to a piece of work may be perceived by the recipient as a significant valuation of them – a valuation which is likely to engender happiness or sadness, acceptance or rejection and so on. Personal experience of grading students and informal observations of others doing this in my own and other HE institutions, suggests that staff can lose confidence in their technical or professional competence to grade and/or feel uncomfortable at being a person who has a legitimate authority to publicly value another person through their work. Academic staff's perception of what is going on, has gone on and what should go on in valuing students' work is worth reporting since it might provide information which can inform staff development programmes in HE, which in turn can play a part in creating or developing productive and convivial work environments for staff and students alike.

More generally, I discuss in Chapter 6 the 'socially responsible university', outlining some perspectives from economics and political philosophy which might begin to offer a theoretical and moral account of the university as an institution. Clearly, in a socially responsible university, a considerable degree of attention will be given to ensure that processes leading to the valuation of people's work are publicly defensible and, just as importantly, that all the internal stakeholders feel comfortable with what goes on. Universities and Colleges significantly improve as institutions when they are successful in increasing the accuracy of the value placed on students' work, and staff and students know that this improvement is taking place. Of course, in the UK and elsewhere, with the increasing emphasis on league tables for teaching quality, there is an increased political and economic motive to be seen to promote student achievement.

The aims of the chapter are, therefore:

1. To suggest that assessment is one of the core activities in HE which any socially responsible university must carry out in a demonstrably accurate and fair-handed way.
2. To contribute to our understanding of academic stress and strain.
3. To explore the contribution which economic theory might make to our understanding of assessment in HE.
4. To report on experiences and perceptions of assessment which might lead to recommendations for changes in assessment processes and procedures and for staff development programmes in order to minimize stress.

ACADEMIC STRESS, STRAIN AND COPING

In 1989, Richard and Krieshok were able to claim that, in developing an understanding of stress: 'the groundwork is still being laid in regard to the definition of stress, individual's reaction to it, and identification of coping methods' (p. 112). An agreed definition of stress is not yet apparent but it is clear that people feel something that can be called stress or they anticipate the threat of stress. A working definition of occupational stress is offered by French (in Gmelch *et al.*, 1984): 'any characteristic of the job environment which poses a threat to the individual – either excessive demands or insufficient supplies to meet his (her) needs' (p. 3). The concept of stress can clearly be highly subjective, with a person's perception of a situation being vital. There will be considerable variation in individual responses to the same or similar situation or conditions (Kahn *et al.*, 1964). The significance of occupational stress, its incidence, intensity and impact, is that it adversely affects the health and happiness of individuals and, subsequently, affects their productivity or performance at work (and elsewhere) and reduces job satisfaction. The bulk of occupational stress studies have focused on employees in the professions, especially the health and caring professions, and the work is dominated by North American studies.

Occupational stress can come from an event which in some way impinges on a person (where the event is a 'stressor') and creates a psychological and physiological response. The amount of stress experienced will depend on the subject's recognition of the 'stressor' and on the adequacy of the person's coping strategies. 'Stress' creates 'strain' to the degree that the person can 'cope'. This three-fold framework has been developed in considerable detail by Osipow and Spokane (1984), and subsequently by Osipow and Davis (1988). The basic theoretical framework here defines stress as an objective environmental characteristic, strain as an individual's subjective response to stress and personal resources as an individual's armoury of coping weapons for dealing with strain.

The measurement of strain is fraught with difficulties. Approaches include psychological and physiological testing, and self-reporting. In any case, theoretically, given equal amounts of stress, strain will be moderated by coping (Richard and Krieshok, 1989). Occupational stress refers to any characteristics of the job environment which threaten a person, characteristics often called stressors, and people cope or not, for example through confronting the stressor or building up the capacity to avoid strain:

> Factors involved in coping include situational constraints, social factors, cultural variations, personality factors, conformity to group pressure, beliefs about what is normally right and wrong, motives and ego resources.   (Goldenberg and Waddell, 1990, p. 533)

Osipow and Davis (1988) examined 'The relationship of coping resources to occupational stress and strain'. They used what is now a well-known measurement method, the Osipow and Spokane (1983) 'Measures of occupational stress, strain and coping'. This has three scales: the occupational environment scale (OES); the personal strain questionnaire (PSQ); and the personal resources questionnaire (PRQ). Each of these scales is constructed on a five-point Likert scale and the summation of ten item scores yields a sub-scale score for a particular variable (Osipow and Davis, 1988).

There is a 'broadly accepted sequence of events depicting the stress process' (Gmelch *et al.*, 1984, p. 474). Gmelch provided a summary of the work of over 1200 academic staff from 80 American universities and found that the sequence or sources of strain were similar to those of other occupations. Generally, the major role stressors are role conflict, role ambiguity, role overload, role insufficiency and responsibility as a burden. Amongst the North American faculty staff, Gmelch found that the sources of stress included:

> excessively high self-expectations, the pressure to secure financial support for research, insufficient time to keep up with developments in the field, inadequate salary, manuscript preparation, role overload, conflicting job demands, slow progress on career advancement, frequent interruptions, and long meetings.   (in Richard and Krieshok, 1989, p. 120)

Of course, as many faculty know to their cost, meetings concerned with assessment are normally the longest of all. There appears to be no greater pleasure in life for some staff but to expound on the inadequacies of the regulations (when, perhaps, a favoured student's qualities are not seen to be reflected by 'the system'), and no greater horror for other staff when a particular hand goes up to attract the attention of the Chair so that a pronouncement on the precise characteristics of a first-class candidate can be made.

The major psychological approach to the analysis and study of occupational stress is to consider stress, strain and coping as a closed, interactive sequence, where strain is a function of stress and coping or, put another way, where exposure to stress or strain will be moderated by coping (Osipow and Davis, 1988). Osipow and Davis claim that 'all coping resources were effective in reducing the global strain' (p. 12) but this seems tautological. Of more interest are their findings that high levels of social support, such as the ability to call on friends and co-workers, high levels of recreation and self-care were all more effective, in different ways, than what they call 'cognitive / rational coping' (p. 12). Nonetheless, it is also the case that, sadly, rivalry between staff, departments and the bureaucracy can create the opposite, where individuals gloat over the mistakes and problems of others. Of course, staff who are reasonably disliked can get their come-uppance on such occasions. Faculty who have to work closely with a member of staff who is arrogantly inefficient and aggressively lazy may deserve the odd, fleeting moment of glee at their colleague's embarrassment before the well-known coping strategy for this sort of individual sets in – namely of believing they are in the company of second-rate people. The stress–strain–coping model, when related to occupational stress, starts with the presumption that the work environment may be a source of physical and psychological stress. The amount of personal strain experienced is influenced by the availability of coping strategies and other personal resources:

> Relatively high stress levels might not be debilitating if a person has adequate resources to handle stress. Low stress levels, however, may be debilitating if personal resources and coping strategies are limited.   (Brown, 1986, p. 98)

Coping strategies can be active or passive. Active strategies aim to confront and eliminate the source of stress and passive strategies aim to strengthen individual resources, although active and passive strategies are not mutually exclusive. Concepts missing in the typical stress–strain–coping model are that of recognition, appraisal or evaluation. These give the situation meaning for the individual (Goldenberg and Waddell, 1990).

Academics in HE have usually claimed that they have a heavy workload, with a complex mixture of role expectations and pressure to maintain professional credibility. Most studies of academic stress, which we have already noted as being dominated by North American accounts, focus on the perception of stress, or on trying to measure the amount of stress that exists and on identifying the sources of stress. Few studies were found which investigated how situational variables may be related to academic stress and strain. This would involve taking a potentially significant aspect of the job itself, such as teaching, research, administration, management or service, and looking within these for key tasks that it could be presumed might be regarded as stressful. For example, the Brown *et al.* (1986) study of 'Stress on campus' found that the time of the year was related to stress, with middle and end of semester times being more stressful than the beginning. Goldenberg and Waddell (1990), after a detailed and interesting study of 'Occupational stress and coping strategies among female baccalaureate nursing faculty', claim that: 'more research in an episodic tradition is necessary. This includes studying actual behaviours as they occur in stressful situations and then inferring coping processes inherent in the behaviour' (p. 541). When Gmelch and associates searched for significant differences in the way academics in different disciplines report and experience stress, they could not find any. Rather, they claim there is: 'strong evidence for the existence of a general, diffuse problem of stress in university settings as opposed to the existence of more discipline-specific problems' (Gmelch *et al.*, 1984, p. 486).

It may be that the metaphysics of university life has an anti-therapeutic effect, compared with, say, workers in manufacturing industry who may not allow any doubts to creep in about the nature and quality of the product they are producing. Academic life is riddled with uncertainty, dilemma and ambiguity by its very nature – questions concerning what counts as good teaching, the relationship between teaching and learning, the presence or otherwise of original work, and questions about whether there is any point at all to HE, can be stressful. (Though answering 'none at all' to the last question can be wonderfully cathartic.) Gmelch's finding does not ignore or refute the possibility that specific aspects of teaching, research, administration, management or service might be experienced very differently by different individuals. Richard and Krieshok (1989), in their study of university faculty in the USA, found a gender–rank–strain relationship: 'Whereas strain decreased for males as they moved up in rank, it tended to increase for females as they were promoted' (p. 128).

One promoted female academic, Shirley Fisher, subtitles her book on *Stress in Academic Life* (1994), *The Mental Assembly Line*. Her work on stress in academic staff leads her to prescribe self-determined work speciality systems (SWS). Here, academics structure their own preferred balance between teaching, administration and research and so on, and negotiate their wishes, within the framework of their contract, with the executive. This is her solution to the problem posed by Professor Graham Hill in his foreword to the book: 'there never was so much paper, so much to know and so much to do'. More specifically, in the USA, Gmelch *et al.* (1984) found that respondents in their study of 'Stress in academe' identified the 'top three stressors' (p. 483) as:

- imposing excessively high self-expectations
- securing financial support for my research
- having insufficient time to keep abreast with current developments in my field

Each of these top three stressors were identified as a considerable source of stress by approximately half of the 800 faculty who completed the survey instrument and, as we have seen, there were no significant differences in response according to the academic discipline of staff. The Gmelch study also explored whether the common major dimensions of teaching, research and administration and service were experienced differently, with respect to reported stress, by faculty and whether disciplinary specialism was significant here in any difference found. No significant differences were found, with each functional category likely to be stressful for any member of faculty. Above all, the Gmelch study emphasizes that what the study calls the 'demanding self-imposed standards' (p. 488) which faculty set for themselves are among the most stress-producing aspects of academic life. Brown *et al.* (1986) found that the most frequently reported sign of stress was some form of body signal, such as a headache. This study involved some 250 US faculty, over 60 per cent of whom reported body signals as their major sign of stress, with other signs, such as changes in mood, including short-temperedness or irritability, reported substantially less frequently. The latter may, of course, be difficult to spot in oneself. Brown *et al.* (1986) found his high 'Role Overload score' mainly determined by lack of time to do jobs well and his low 'Social Support' score significantly determined by faculty, finding other people as a source of stress (as well, of course, as a source of support).

In one of the rare studies of faculty stress in Further Education in the UK, John Snape (1992) identified four potential stressors for lecturers: 'Lack of recognition, poor resource facilities, relationships with students and lack of money for resources' (p. 29). His 'mediators' are personal characteristics, for example, 'hardiness' and the nature of the 'Home-College Interface' (p. 29). In an interesting discussion, Snape speculates on the outcomes of the traditional stress–strain–coping interactive relationship amongst staff in FE. His analysis suggests a number of positions following a stressful experience, where FE faculty:

• perceive they are coping and performance is not affected
• perceive they are not coping and performance is not affected
• perceive they are not coping and performance is affected (improved or made worse?)

ECONOMIC THEORY, DECISION-MAKING AND ASSESSMENT IN HE

Snape was particularly concerned with teaching performance but I want to turn now to the specific issue of assessment of students' work as a function which academics have to carry out. Increasingly, academics formally assess other academics as part of internal or external review and appraisal. Processes of student assessment affect the life chances of students and affect them as people. The ability to assess students' work also affects the life chances of lecturers. Assessment might be a strain on both student and lecturer, and could lead to stress so this has to be dealt with for well-being. One way into a description and analysis of staff–student relationships in the context of the assessment process has been studies which have examined aspects of the growth of student appraisal of lecturer quality. For example, is student appraisal of lecturer quality linked in any significant way to the grades which students are given by the lecturer being appraised? Do students tend to approve of staff who give them good marks? The evidence is inconclusive, with a great deal of inconsistency in the findings. Some studies find significant positive ratings between student grades and faculty rating while others do not. It has also proved difficult to disentangle the propositions, first, that students who learn more rank their lecturers higher and second, that lecturers buy high ratings through giving students high grades (Feldman, 1976; Perkins *et al.*, 1990).

In the Feldman study, student ranking of staff was significantly related to whether the student received a higher mark than they expected to achieve. The concept of 'grade discrepancy' (Feldman, p. 636) is interesting because of its possible link to a coping strategy for dealing with expected strain. Grade discrepancies exist where the grade the student expects is lower than the grade assigned by staff. Everyone here is happy and the inducement to grade high (on balance, to play safe, on certain types of courses, with particular students or groups of students) is evident and even clearer when tied to possible security, income or promotion for staff because of the influence of student appraisal reports in influencing faculty careers. Of course, what the student expects from a particular member of staff is affected by whether the member of staff is seen as 'easy', 'fair' or 'hard' in their assessment of students' work. Hard markers who give high marks now and then may receive very high ratings from the limited number of students who experience this. Easy staff who give, occasionally, low marks may be condemned. The general point here is that the process of assigning a grade by faculty to students is an interactive activity, the more so when students have powers in ranking or otherwise grading staff. The decision to give a grade matters to all parties so stress and strain seems likely.

If people want to be popular, they can both refuse to differentiate between students and simultaneously award high marks across the board. This might be easier to do where there is a general perception that the marking has to be very subjective, for example on Fine Art degree courses, where the quality of the product is inevitably seen to be contentious and where it may be thought that like cannot be compared with like; or, despite OFSTED, in marking the teaching practice component of, say, students training to be Physical Education teachers, where the attitude of the student may be foremost in the valuation. One insecure history teacher in a Cornish Comprehensive school once gave an 'A' grade to all members of her 'difficult' class of 15-year-olds to curry favour/ avoid hassle, to the derision of all concerned. Does something similar ever happen in HE? In a College of Education in the West Midlands during the late 1960s, a philosophy of education lecturer who did not believe in assessment at all, but had to produce marks to feed into a degree classification process, told his final year students that he was submitting a list of marks which showed all students performing at the mid-lower second class honours category, at 55. This caused the Head of Department some difficulties and led to considerable stress for the students. On a one-year taught Master of Arts programme at a well known Dutch university, the lecturer submitted a mark of 100 per cent for all the students except one. When the student drew the Head of Department's attention to this, it became clear that the students were marked for attendance. Attendance at the ten sessions had been staggeringly high, except for this one unfavoured student whose late arrival for class, because her car lift had not turned up, had been gleefully reflected in the 90 per cent mark.

A study by Pambookian (1976) starts from the proposition that faculty self-ratings of performance are normally a good indicator of performance – staff who claim to be good teachers are usually ranked by others as good teachers. Pambookian examined a different form of discrepancy than Feldman by looking at where student ranking or grading of faculty was at variance with faculty grading of themselves. Pambookian's study was concerned, in part, with examining the concept of cognitive dissonance. Faculty with high self-ranking were expected to experience cognitive dissonance if they were subject to lower than expected student ranking of their performance. The study's central hypothesis was that: 'the greater the discrepancy between instructor self-evaluation and students' evaluations of instruction, the greater is the change (i.e. improvement) after feedback' (p. 65). It follows that the greater the magnitude of discrepancy or dissonance, the greater is the pressure on faculty to reduce it, whether the discrepancy be negative (unfavourable) or positive (favourable), according to Pambookian. This approach has its problems. For example, where a lecturer ranks themself low but the students rank them high, there seems little incentive to 'reduce' the discrepancy. The elation might offset the dissonance. Nonetheless, some sort of drive for equilibrium or accuracy in perception, or search for balance or symmetry suggests a link with stress, strain and coping. Theories of consistency, claims Pambookian, quoting McGuire (1966), have in common the notion that the person: 'Tends to behave in ways to minimise the internal inconsistency among his interpersonal relations, among his interpersonal cognitions, or among his beliefs, feelings, and actions' (p. 65).

What then do students think is a fair grade? They probably know that much assessment is subjective even though there are forms of assessment which are more objective than others. Subjective judgements are value judgements and Parducci (Wedell *et al.*, 1989) has utilized range-frequency theory to propose that value judgements, such as assigning a grade, represent a compromise between a range and a frequency principle. We can add that if the outcome of a grading process is perceived by all parties to be fair, even though the process of reaching this position may be a strain, the outcome is stress-free. An example of what is known as a 'straight' scale within the range principle is the grading system, in common use in British higher education, where a range, say 0–100, is divided into equal sub-ranges, say 0–10, 10–20, and so on and a letter grade attached to each sub-range. Here the grade cut-offs are independent of the frequency distribution of scores. The frequency principle suggests a scale where an equal number of scores is attached to each category. For example, those scores which come in the top 20 per cent of the array of scores are given an 'A' grade. Under the range principle, only scores above, say, 90 would be given an 'A' grade (i.e. no scores may achieve an 'A' grade whereas under a frequency principle grade system, the top fifth say, of all scores would be given an 'A'). This discussion simply shows that different systems of grading exist, that faculty either choose or are party to a choice which results in one sort of system or other, or a combined system. Which of these three possibilities is perceived to be the fairest? The study by Wedell *et al.* (1989) found that a combined range–frequency system was seen by students to be fairest; that is, the students assumed a normal curve of distribution. There would always be some 'A's from this system, but not too many.

We have asked, what do students think is a fair grade? We also need to raise the same question on behalf of employers. One of the major criticisms from employers or potential employers of university graduates is that there is too much uncertainty about what an actual grade, award or classification means. What does it signify that people are good at, or rather, in what way and to what extent do credentials predict an employee's productive contribution to an employing organization? What employers want, for the least possible search costs, and subsequent labour costs, is to get their hands on the most potentially productive graduates of educational systems (see Chapter 1, pp. 12–13). Assessment of performance by educational systems is a major subsidy to company labour search costs only as far as the legitimation by educational bodies of people's abilities, through credentials via assessment, can be trusted, and that similar awards, say upper second class honours degrees in history from different universities, do indicate a comparable range and level of abilities. The search should be to provide a generally convincing system of credentialism that is transparently fair, which would eliminate false senses of achievement and competence for all people with a stake in the process of assessment.

Economists are interested in getting the best outcome from the least cost. Economics is about getting rid of waste (Baumol, 1991). Students impose potentially major costs on university assessment, classification and certification systems when they feel they should question a mark because they disagree with the grade, presumably thinking it an unfair reflection of their ability (being out of keeping with their personal self-rating of ability or not conforming to their perception of the faculty as easy, hard or fair). Economists refer to such costs as transaction costs and except for situations where transaction time is actually a benefit, for example, the case for some British tourists when 'haggling' over prices in North African street markets, these costs are usually kept to a minimum. (It may also be the case that grade bargaining is akin to haggling, but this is probably rare.) What faculty certainly want most, if not all, of the time is a system of grade assignment which is either transparently fair, or not open to discussion. The former is difficult to achieve, given, as we have seen, the subjective nature of grading, and the latter, in 1996, would be politically unacceptable in the UK (see the Student's Charter). The use of external examiners as independent arbiters has been a traditional way of ensuring a fair final solution to the risky business of assessing human abilities and the contribution which teaching or lecturing makes to this. However, external examiners are individuals who may be riddled with self-doubt or misconceived confidence within their own institutions and it seems unlikely that they offer further objectivity or accuracy to the valuing process in universities. Rather, they seem more like a novice counsellor from Relate, desperately trying to be an accurate reader, an attentive and sympathetic listener, and to enable all parties to save face if at all possible.

'What we need is a strategy for dealing in a serious, judicious and seemingly fair and responsive way' (Goldfarb, 1994) with heart-felt and arguably legitimate complaints about grading. Such a strategy may lead to strain and stress reduction in academic life. Academic staff working within such a system would have more chance of avoiding being labelled a 'hard' or 'difficult' marker and, probably more heinous in the eyes of other faculty, being seen as an 'easy touch'. What we want is a system where, as a result of grade transaction between faculty and student, both benefit. This would result in a Pareto improvement in welfare. Goldfarb (1994), Professor of Economics at George Washington University, suggests that students will feel better (stress reduction in our terms) as a result of the process of appropriate reconsideration of a grade, and faculty will feel better through demonstrating their humanity and/or because it may lead to a more accurate signal of the student's performance. Of course, as in Parliamentary lobbying, there is a danger that access to negotiation is biased towards the rich and powerful, or in this case, the good or beautiful. In the film *Scent of a Woman*, the boys at the American elite private college felt immune from the tyranny of faculty judgements because they could call on the counter tyranny of their fathers who were paying the inflated fees.

Goldfarb was concerned with exam grades and 'arguably legitimate exam gripes' but his technique could be adopted to deal with course work issues as well. What he suggests is a two-fold process. Students can put in writing their reasons for believing that the grade they received is unfair. These concerns are not dealt with immediately but, given the nature of the grading system, say, at the end of a semester, the student's comments are seriously considered where an upward adjustment would make a difference to the student's overall profile. For some students or for some particular assignments, Goldfarb's technique will not suffice. The period of waiting for possible review may itself lead to stress and there are situations where the actual piece of work has to receive a fair mark, irrespective of its possible overall insignificance in determining a final classification of some sort. For example, a philosophy student studying the work of Emmanuel Kant who cannot seem to understand Kant, as evidenced by the presentation of a lowly graded, fairly marked, first essay, who believes that the second essay on Kant suggests that she has finally understood Kant, will want the grading of her level of understanding, as shown in the second essay, to be fair. She needs to know whether she has understood Kant correctly or not for her own peace of mind or self-development.

The process of assigning a grade involves a choice within an allocation system of grades. Economists are very interested in choice, preference and risk, and have lived, until recently, with a much criticized but difficult to supersede 'neo-classical', stable preference approach to economic theory: 'Economic man, rational without thought, without morals, moral dilemmas, hesitation or indecision, has rightly been the object of many lampoons' (McCain, 1990, p. 125).

McCain attempts to develop an alternative theory of economic choice, what he calls 'impulse-filtering' (p. 126). His analysis is applicable to the grading process and, I believe, offers a philosophical account of economic choice and insights into the well known philosophical problem of the freedom of the will. His analysis can be applied to the particular value judgement which is of concern here, namely, the choice of grade, and McCain's analysis is elegant and illuminative. He suggests that the basic economic choice is a binary one: this or that, yes or no, as in the decision to award one grade rather than any other. How do we arrive at a decision? In McCain's model, we are influenced by the 'interaction of a stream of *impulses* with a system of *filters*' (p. 126*)*. We know that the impulses are in part random and this accords with the subjective aspect of the decision to grade. The filters determine whether the impulse is acted on or not, but, of course, the filters may suggest mutually inconsistent actions. In neo-classical economics, the importance of the concept of utility is derived from the assumption that we can compare all possible choices and reduce them to a common preference ordering. All possible alternatives are then arrayed with the most preferred acted on. However, in real life, we know that people ponder for an indecisive period, not able to make a choice, and faculty ponder over a grade allocation. If all assessment is reduced to item analysis marking, according to a schedule agreed by appropriate faculty, then a computer can do the job though people will still have to deal with feedback, in general, and gripes in particular (though this might be hived off to the student counselling service or personal tutor system).

On coursework, the students usually receive written justifications for the grade, often in relation to set of assessment criteria – originality, analysis, use of language, coverage, and so on. Then the door is wide open for anxiety arising from the perceived incongruence of the written comments and the actual grade given. This is more likely where faculty are encouraged to be positive and diagnostic in their comments, seeking to praise strengths and to suggest ways of eliminating weakness. On the other hand, given faculty work overload, the paucity of comments can lead to anxiety and distress for the student, and ultimately strain for the lecturer, because the student does not know why the piece of work was graded the way it was, but is determined to find out and is prepared to bear the search costs. Where assessment criteria are of different kinds (analysis, compared to coverage), reducing complex subjective evaluations to a single grade is clearly, at best, a least worst way of doing things. Even where faculty have access to a weighted set of criteria, they may still feel uncomfortable and even reject the guidelines. If they do the latter, presumably they should not be involved in the assessment process. Disputes over criteria are more likely on modular schemes, where staff who may know little of the approach of other staff, nonetheless find themselves teaching on and assessing modules which are shared by students and team-taught by staff who have different perceptions of what a fair assessment procedure looks like.

The choice to assign one grade rather than any other is a choice made under risk. The decision may create transaction costs, through student complaint or attempts to negotiate, or may lead to insecurity, where the licence to grade is undermined by some perception of the probability of getting things wrong. (And, maybe, being embarrassed by the decision of an external examiner to change the grade.) The risks will need to be calculated and, in McCain's model, this involves a cognitive filter. There are risks in being generous – 'easy' marker criticisms from other staff, and in being 'hard' and thereby dismissive of well intentioned people's best efforts. Where a slightly higher number mark will lead to a significantly better letter mark, and given perceptions of the limits of accuracy and expertise with a grading system, it may be difficult to resist going for the mark which is higher than the impulse suggests. This is the cognitive filter working. This in turn may be overlaid with other sorts of filters such as the multiple rose-tinted affective domain filter.

How might this work? Imagine a piece of coursework, say a dissertation, where the student has made it quite clear that she needs a first-class mark to achieve a first overall. She is a mature student, poor, like most, and has been evicted from her flat with her two young children, by a disreputable landlord, and at the time of finishing the dissertation, is living in cramped conditions with another kind-hearted student who has offered temporary shelter. She does not go to the student counselling service but staff know that the dissertation may not 'do the student justice'. One member of staff, the second marker of the dissertation is particularly keen to have the student return as a research student and a first-class mark is essential for applying for Research Council Funding. The first marker's impulse is to mark at 66, a very strong upper second but clearly not a first. The second marker's impulse is the same, but then other filters come into play which persuade the second marker to add in marks for 'circumstances'. The first marker is prepared for this reaction and is even more concerned not to be bargained up so a particularly tight defence is built through the first marker's comments on the script. The first marker may be normally either easy, normal or hard but in this case is hard. The second marker is known to be easy in particular cases, especially where she takes on the role of sponsoring the interests of students who, in her opinion, through no fault of their own, are unfairly disadvantaged by 'circumstance' and/or the 'system'. The final agreed internal mark is 67. The external examiner, new to the job, decides, a week or so later, that all dissertations have been slightly undermarked and raises the mark to 70. The student is deliriously happy.

Similarly, student evaluations of faculty teaching effectiveness and the link between these evaluations and grades awarded by particular staff, can be understood within an analysis of the inadequacies of the economist's neo-classical choice theory. Students may be indecisive, confronted with mutually inconsistent staff impulses (be generous in evaluating they will say, she is basically a decent human being; be responsible in evaluating they add because the future welfare of other students is at stake). The growth of student valuations of faculty is clearly the outcome of the same political pressures which produced the consumer movement of the early 1970s. It is hard to find any research into their reliability and validity (Weinbach, 1988) but it is clear that faculty can and do go to extraordinary lengths to influence student evaluations and the costs of this may be seen in the bureaucracy of quality assurance systems and in activities which may get in the way of good teaching, administration or research: 'Who of us has not, on occasion, assessed the impact on our evaluations of awarding a low grade or confronting a disruptive or truant student?' (Weinbach, 1988, p. 28).

Weinbach was particularly interested in the ways in which faculty manipulate students so as to achieve high rankings on student evaluations. Here we have an interesting interactive process where faculty grades its students and the nature of the faculty grading influences the way in which they in turn get graded by students, that is, where student evaluation systems are in place and they matter. Courses can be made easy and entertaining, with reduced content and lowered grading standards, all of which appear to make courses more popular. It may be that more popular behaviours and less unpopular behaviours are congruent with better teaching and more appropriate learning. Certainly, faculty could learn how to achieve high student evaluations as well as ensure effective teaching but the costs may be high and it may be simpler to take the decision to become popular and discount the impact this might have on student learning. Weinbach (1988) offers 46 different ways, within seven categories, through which faculty can manipulate student evaluations of themselves. On the stress and assessment theme, these include:

6.   Curve exams that generate less than 70% 'A's. It must have been your fault for making the exam excessively rigorous ... Always allow credit for at least one wrong answer to admit your error in question construction.

7.   Re-schedule exams on demand. It helps if other faculty 'rigidly' refuse to give one early so a student can get in on a great rate on a pre-holiday cruise.

10.   Personally call your students to assure them that they did all right on an exam (p. 32)

American university students certainly expect to be in control of their own learning. With tenure and promotion largely dependent on research output, or any measure of performance other than the quality of teaching, faculty have few incentives to bear information dissemination costs except where student evaluations count in the tenure and promotion competitions. One brave junior member of staff at an American University in Indiana was once seen to control an unruly lecture audience, who thought her lecture had gone over time (it was 5 minutes to the end of the session), and where the students, all 500 or so of them, had begun packing their bags to leave, by threatening the students with an extra assessment if they did not hear her out. In any case, her technical assistant finished the session early by switching off her lapel microphone. He was not going to miss lunch.

Are academics good at assessment? Or, in the language of McCain's (1990) revisionist economic theory, how good are they at making choices which are characterized by risk and uncertainty, and by an impulse-filter sequence which may lead to mutually exclusive or paradoxical outcomes? Put another way, how much freedom do faculty have to do the right thing as far as student grading is concerned? We do have some studies of the validity of self-ratings of abilities and competencies (Lowman and Williams, 1987). The classic approach is to use a measure of ability such as the Holland 'Self-Directed Search', or SDS (Lowman and Williams, 1987). Unfortunately, studies of faculty self-ratings, which were compared with some objective measures of competence, proved elusive. If faculty are good at assessment, and there may be good reason to think that they should be good at it, then they should not have to worry too much about it. Let us assume, though, that all faculty, within the limits of the popularity filter, have an impulse to be fair in their grading of students. What can be done to improve the chances of this happening?

EXPERIENCES AND PERCEPTIONS OF ASSESSMENT

The assessment of students' work may be an uncomfortable activity for faculty and students alike, although it may lead to a point of mutual congratulation where the lecturer meets the student's expectation of a very high mark. So far, we have dealt with reporting on some theory which may be appropriate, that is, on the framework of stress, strain and coping, on this threesome in higher education and we have had a brief flirtation with economic theory. Some personal experiences of assessment have also been described and all academics can tell tales about assessment procedures, outcomes and staff–student interactions around the assessment process. What we now need, because it appears to be lacking, is some further work on what it is about the assessment process that makes faculty feel uncomfortable or uneasy, even upset and angry. The beginning point for this chapter was a lecturer who wrote to all staff expressing his disquiet at the procedures and outcomes of an exam board for final year undergraduates. He felt that justice had not been done but had felt helpless to affect the decisions in the presence of his Head of Department, external examiners, other colleagues and senior staff from the university's registry. What we need to do is to try and capture those occasions when faculty feel that things may not be going as they should in their assessment activities and responsibilities and what they do about that – that is, their coping strategies. Critical incident analysis may allow us to do this. One of the main benefits of critical incident analysis is that the reality of work is made vivid. It can produce 'real life' material which people can consider when they are looking at ways of improving their own practice, for example, through a staff development programme. Critical incident analysis can also offer role play situations. Its main contribution to improving ability and confidence in job settings, and hence possibly reducing strain, is that it is problem-centred and focuses on problem-solving strategies:

> Thus, even in negative incidents, the incident reporter can usually come away with feeling good about some of their behaviour and empowered to cope with the incident should it arise again, as a result of identifying other coping strategies through discussion of the incident.
> (MaClachlan and McAucliffe, 1993, p. 10)

One of the major potential uses of critical incident analysis is to create materials for simulation, for example, simulations used in employee selection. These typically present applicants with a task stimulus that mimics an actual situation (Dunnette *et al.*, 1990, pp. 640–7). The responses which potential employees make are then interpreted as direct indicators of how people would handle the situation if it were actually to occur. What critical incident analysis offers this process is a tool for identifying those aspects of a job, or, more generally, a situation, which people tend to find problematic. In the study by Wetchler and Vaughan (1991) which used critical incident analysis, they were concerned with reporting critical incidents in supervision which were claimed to have had a positive effect on the performance of American marriage and family therapy trainees whilst on supervised work experience. In McCain's (1990) scheme, problematic situations arise when the impulse-filter-cognitive appraisal process leads to ambiguity, paradox, or contradiction, or, less dramatically, no clear signals for which choice to make or how to act. We could say to a worker, as part of a critical incident analysis of an occupation, 'tell me about an occasion in your work when you were unsure about what to do next', and stand back to avoid the avalanche.

The seminal article on the critical incident technique appeared in the *Psychological Bulletin*, July 1954. Flanagan's article reports on ten years of development by him and his collaborators. He states that the critical incident technique:

> consists of a set of procedures for collecting direct observations of human behaviour in such a way as to facilitate their potential usefulness in solving practical problems ... [it] outlines procedures for collecting observed incidents having special significance. By an incident is meant any observable human activity that is sufficiently complete in itself to permit inferences and predictions to be made about the person performing the act. To be critical, an incident must occur in a situation where the purpose or intent of the act seems fairly clear to the observer and where its consequences are sufficiently definite to leave little doubt concerning its effects. (Flanagan, 1954, p. 327)

Early studies were concerned with life and death situations, for example, analysis of the specific reasons why trainees pilots failed to learn to fly, where army officers failed to develop the critical requirements of combat leadership, and why air traffic controllers, dentists and surgeons made mistakes. One study (Smit, 1952) tried to determine the critical requirements for instructors of general psychology courses. The instructors reported behaviours largely to do with teaching methods whereas the students were largely concerned with processes for reviewing examinations, distributing grades and explaining grades:

> Examination of the reports from students indicated a somewhat limited sphere of competence. Apparently one of the principal reasons for this was the lack of perspective on the part of the students and their inability to keep the general aim of their instructor clearly in mind because of its divergence from their own immediate aims. In many cases, this latter aim seemed to be directed toward achieving a satisfactory grade in the course. (Flanagan, 1954, p. 334)

Flanagan seems unnecessarily limiting in his response to Smit's work. Staff may still become very defensive when faced with a request for a review or some other form of opening of negotiations around a grade or classification. They may even, in my experience, become aggressive with the student and undermine the student's abilities or personality with colleagues. One strong-minded physical education student, for example, who would not buy his track suit from the recommended (College) shop, believed that his work would therefore be constantly undervalued and subsequently left the course, which, of course, is exactly what some staff wanted. A socially responsible university would develop processes within the university which allow assessment decisions to be reviewed in a meaningful way and which ensure that providing feedback on the reasons for assessment decisions is always available to avoid uncertainty; and where the risk of intimidation by staff of students and students of staff is minimized. Such information and transaction costs are worth bearing. Today, as we have noted, faculty may have little choice, given changes in the relative power of students and staff in the determination of grades, but to become focused on grading processes and outcomes. Similarly, even the most deferent or disinterested of students may come under severe peer group pressure to complain and seek justice and even redress, or compensation.

The core of the critical incident technique is that it is a procedure for gathering certain important facts concerning behaviour in defined situations. It is not a rigid set of rules but rather a flexible set of principles (Flanagan, 1954, p. 335). The situation I am interested in is when academic staff have to grade students' work. What do staff report that they do in order to arrive at a grade, which of those activities appears to cause them difficulty, and how do they report that they deal with the difficulty? How comfortable do faculty in HE in the UK feel with grading processes and outcomes? Generally, we know both an awful lot and very little about faculty and students' management of assessment in British higher education. Those who work in HE or are students know, as do their nearest and dearest, that feelings can run high when assessed work is returned to students. But we know little, apart from personal experience, about the degree of confidence that faculty feel in valuing another human being's work, and the meaning and significance of this work, both in terms of the stress, strain and coping impacts and strategies or through the application of some analytical framework, such as economic theory. Such inquiries would help fill the gaps we have in our understanding of what HE is really all about, what there is about it that makes participants happy and sad and what power it has to promote human and social development. Researching the stress and strain arising from the social, technical and legal aspects of assessment may in itself be a successful coping strategy.

REFERENCES

Baumol, W. (1991) *Perfect Markets and Easy Virtue*. Oxford: Blackwell.

Brown, R.D. *et al.* (1986) 'Stress on campus: an interactional perspective.' *Research in Higher Education*, **24**(1), 97–112.

Dunnette, M.D., Motowidio, G.J. and Carter, G.W. (1990) 'An alternative selection procedure: the low-fidelity simulation'. *Journal of Applied Psychology*, **75**(6), 620–47.

Feldman, K.A. (1976) 'Grades and college students' evaluations of their course and teachers'. *Research in Higher Education*, **4**(1), 69–111.

Fisher, S. (1994) *Stress in Academic Life*. Milton Keynes: Open University Press.

Flanagan, J.C. (1954) 'The Critical Incident Technique'. *Psychological Bulletin*, **51**(4), 327–58.

Gmelch, W.H. *et al.* (1984) 'Sources of stress in academe: a national perspective'. *Research in Higher Education*, **20**(4), 477–90.

Goldenberg, D. and Waddell, J. (1990) 'Occupational stress and coping strategies among female baccalaureate nursing faculty'. *Journal of Advanced Nursing*, **15**, 531–43.

Goldfarb, R.S. (1994) 'Dealing with arguably legitimate exam gripes: a possible Pareto improvement'. *Economic Inquiry*, **32**, 178–9.

Kahn, R.L. *et al.* (1964) *Organizational Stress: Studies in Role Conflict and Ambiguity*. Chichester: J. Wiley.

Lowman, R.L. and Williams, R.E. (1987) 'Validity of self-ratings of abilities and competencies'. *Journal of Vocational Behaviour*, **31**, 1–13.

MaClachlan, M. and McAucliffe, E. (1993) 'Critical incidents for psychology students in a refugee camp: implications for counselling'. *Counselling Psychology Quarterly*, **6**(1), 3–11.

McCain, R.A. (1990) 'Impulse-filtering: a new model of freely willed economic choice'. *Review of Social Economy*, **48**, 125–43.

McGuire, W.J. (1966) 'The current status of cognitive consistency theories'. In Feldman, S. (ed.) *Cognitive Consistency: Motivational Antecedents and Behavioral Consequents*. London: Academic Press.

Osipow, S.H. and Davis, A.S. (1988) 'The relationship of coping resources to occupational stress and strain'. *Journal of Vocational Behaviour*, **32**, 1–15.

Osipow, S.H. and Spokane, A.R. (1984) 'Measuring occupational stress, strain and coping'. In Oskamp, S. (ed.) *Applied Social Psychology Annual*. Vol. 5. Beverley Hills: Sage.

Pambookian, H.S. (1976) 'Discrepancy between instructor and student evaluations of instruction: effect on instructor'. *Instructional Science*, **5**, 63–75.

Perkins, D., Guerin, D. and Schleh, J. (1990) 'Effects of grading standard information, assigned grade, and grade discrepancies on students' evaluations'. *Psychological Reports*, **66**, 635–42.

Richard, G.V. and Krieshok, T.S. (1989) 'Occupational stress, strain and coping in university faculty'. *Journal of Vocational Behaviour*, **34**, 117–32.

Smit, J. (1952) 'A study of the critical requirements for instructors of general psychology courses'. *University of Pittsburg Bulletin*, **48**.

Snape. J. (1992) 'Stress in lecturers: A proposed theoretical model for the further education arena'. *Education Today*, **42**(4), 26–31.

The Student's Charter (1993) London: HMSO.

Wedell, D.H., Parducci, A. and Roman, D. (1989) 'Student perceptions of fair grading: a range-frequency analysis'. *American Journal of Psychology*, **102**(2), 233–48.

Weinbach, R.W. (1988) 'Manipulations of student evaluations: No laughing matter'. *Journal of Social Work Education*, **24**(Winter) 27–34.

Wetchler, J. and Vaughan, K.A. (1991) 'Perceptions of primary supervisor interpersonal skills: a critical incident analysis'. *Contemporary Family Therapy*, **13**(1), 61–9.

Chapter 6

The Socially Responsible University

INTRODUCTION

The main argument presented here is that the best possible relationship between the university and its area of benefit cannot be defined and worked for until a clearer picture emerges of exactly what a university is and what it should be for. The move in universities towards missions, codes of conduct, quality guarantees and other sorts of public statements about aims and obligations has arisen out of an administrative need to establish external accountability criteria and internal control mechanisms. What is required is a parallel movement which takes stock of developments in appropriate disciplines and sub-disciplines in order to apply these to create insights into what the university currently is and what it might be. That is, we need an academic account of university life as well as a manager's account.

This chapter is concerned with exploring the nature of the university as a social organization, and as an institution, in order to provide some benchmarks for how the organisation should relate to its area of benefit. The proposition presented, in a brief, is that there is still much work to be done on the nature of the university as an organization and a good starting place for analysis is to assert a preference for how the university should be, that is, it should be socially responsible, or, to use a more contentious label, it should exhibit political correctness. Like any complex and influential organization, asking questions about general purpose and establishing arguments about entitlements to exist and to flourish will suggest a wide range of complementary and contrasting answers (Allen and Martin, 1992). However, it is still possible to work in a university and remain insensitive to or to be excluded from institutional debates about what the organization should be for, and how it might shift from what it is and has been to what it might and should be.

The focus of the discussion will be to suggest that the theory and practice of university education is still susceptible to the long-standing critique that universities have failed to meet the needs of industry. Perspectives from economic and political theory might be useful in identifying an appropriate response to this widespread and important criticism. We need to work at creating a political economy of the university within a clear ethical framework. This is what is taken here to be the meaning of 'political correctness'. This will require engaging with some aspects of political and moral philosophy as applied to an understanding of liberal, democratic societies and using appropriate perspectives from the economics of the firm and from business ethics. The assertion is that such academic frameworks are available and yet have been under-used in analysing the nature of the university (and educational institutions in general). No attempt is made in the chapter to think through their application in depth but rather examples are given which hopefully hint at the possible contribution these perspectives can offer.

There is a powerful lobby which has argued that the university sector must be more like industry. Oddly, this crude claim has received little academic attention in the sense that neither the type of industry nor the exact nature of the specific firm within the model industry is usually specified. The argument remains at a political level only, as a vivid symbol of the failings of universities, and as an affirmation of a claim that any firm is likely to be more useful and to be a greater contributor to the common good, than any university. What is long overdue is an identification and analysis of those firms which are, say, efficient at producing useful goods through democratically constructed worker relationships, and see how different universities compare with this template.

Traditionally, organizations are categorized by economists and public policy analysts as being located within the private, public or voluntary sectors, or at the smallest unit of sectoral division. Families or individuals are categorized as organizations in themselves. Employed individuals belong to at least two sectors, the family or individual and one other. This sectoral location framework stresses differences in ownership, management and regulation according to placing. Where does the university reside? It would be very helpful if we could feel confident that this sectoral division is analytically powerful. Simultaneously, if we could agree on the basic defining characteristics of the university, then location within the framework would be most helpful in answering our naive question, what is a university? When we move from the empirical to the preferential and ask what a university should be, it would be equally useful to say that we know what a good firm is and the university should be more like that than it is. This position accepts that the industrial critique of the university has been the strongest force for change. Moreover, this critique, that universities have failed to meet the needs of the nation and its citizens because they have not met the needs of industry, and, by extension, should become an active part of industry, is not new. As long as there has been publicly financed higher education in the UK, there has been a dominant lobby of critics who have used the argument about failure to meet the needs of industry as a stick to beat the universities into their rightful place and function (Aronowitz and Giroux, 1985). So we have had two dynamics, the evolution of higher education and the evolution of industry with the latter being used politically as the role model for the former.

All this is well known and yet, as has been hinted, remains elusive as an intellectual argument. We need more work on the political economy of the university if we are to be able to produce a convincing brief for how the university should be in relation to its area of benefit. The political analysis is more in place than the economic analysis. Morgan's work (1986) on the political images of organizations offers concepts and schemes for making good sense of the power structure of organizations and Harris (1990) has put together a useful dialogue on the concept of political obligation, which, as we shall see, will be needed to focus the discussion on the individual and the organization. However, I want now to focus on the contribution that new perspectives from managerial economics and business ethics might make in contributing to locating the university within an appropriate framework of description and analysis. These two accounts of the university can be merged in order to ask whether universities are socially responsible, and if so, in what sense? We can take the view, accepting the historical critique of higher education, that this is a very similar question to asking whether firms are socially responsible. This line of approach indicates that firms themselves have been under intense scrutiny by academics working within the emerging disciplines of managerial economics and business ethics, and this scrutiny has added to the political pressure on universities to reconstruct themselves in the light of their regretful unintended contribution to Britain's economic decline (Gamble, 1986).

ECONOMIC AND POLITICAL THEORY

Economic sub-systems are found at the level of the individual, the firm and the state and a super-economic system both conditions and emerges from the economic activities of the sub-systems. IBM, part of the super-system and one of the world's largest and most well known companies, has shifted from being a paragon of how a firm should be organized and how it should behave, to a horror story of how things can go badly wrong (Reich, 1993). IBM is now perceived as having an expensive plant and assembly structure, a 'fat' middle management and an inability to lead or stay up with product innovation. The solutions suggested indicate the managerial correct solution of our times – a slimmer HQ, more local autonomy and control and a different and greater valuation of human resources.

In the UK, British Airways, 'the world's favourite airline', authorized its staff to poach customers from Virgin and to discredit Virgin, to attack its squeaky clean image, through what was claimed to be a dirty tricks campaign. In Oliver Stone's film *Wall Street*, the USA captain of industry, played by Michael Douglas, tries to 'out' dirty trick the English captain of industry, played by Terence Stamp. Firms, if caught out, can now expect the media (unless it is a media organization itself under ethical inquisition) to fuel a critique of the firm not on its falling productivity or market share or profit level, but on its level of morality. And we have Greenpeace as the major moral guardians of corporate and government activities, as Shell and the French government have experienced in recent years.

Lately it has been possible to link the focus of attention on business morality in the UK to the importation of American business techniques following the 1980s stock market boom which dramatically increased the number of American firms located in the City of London, together with the growth of financial and public relations firms and the emergence of 'deal-doers', 'movers and shakers' and 'spin merchants'. Notably, British Airways has never publicly acknowledged any conduct of which it is ashamed. There seems to be a wide gap between what the owners and managers of firms define as legitimate activity and the perception and expectation of the general public. For Richard Branson, the aggrieved major shareholder in Virgin, BA's actions went 'beyond any limits of commercially acceptable practice' (Kane, 1993).

It may well be, as the French radical economist and active green politician, Lipietz (1992) has argued, that teamwork is shaping the twenty-first century in the same way as time and motion shaped the twentieth century but teamwork is not an end in itself. It seems inadequate to applaud the emergence of seemingly convivial work relationships without ensuring they are directed towards some desirable product – here, process cannot be subsumed by the importance of product, or vice versa.

Is there, then, a 'new culture at large in the boardroom' (Brummer 1993) or the Senate? Following fundamental changes in the management and organization of ICI in the UK, Brummer argues that these decisions are part of a much bigger change in the way that the corporate world manages itself. ICI, in the immediate post-war period, acted as a large corporation, with transnational interests, but clearly having a national identity and an obligation to behave in the national interest, indeed, to be part of the national interest. International economic forces, such as the globalization of production, a less centralized and more autonomous local style of management and the impact of rapid advances in communications technology, have gone hand in glove with new or higher profile responsibilities. Companies such as ICI in Britain, VW in Germany and Sony in Japan no longer simply represent the interests of share holders and investors. Local and national economies and, more metaphysically, the environment and the future, claim corporate obligations from these companies. Companies are reorganizing both industrially and ethically. Lord King was required to retire early as chairman of British Airways after the exposure of the claimed dirty tricks campaign against Virgin, yet could point to major financial successes for BA in an industry characterized by massive debt liabilities and major profit losses. Companies can no longer trade off ethical concerns against financial needs with impunity.

Reich (1993) has argued that corporate nationality has become irrelevant. The common strand in business success, for Reich, is the ability to secure the skills and insights necessary to sustain industrial innovation which should include, we now know, the skills and insights to identify, prioritize and deliver a range of corporate responsibilities. President Clinton, in his first major economic policy speech, stressed the theme of national renewal, urging a strengthening and affirmation of patriotism. This speech may well have been influenced by the need to assert publicly the role of the state as a countervailing power to the rise of foot-loose and nation-free corporations. The theme is also underwritten by the long-standing issue of protectionism. So, populations within nation states are faced with what looks like an increasing vacuum in their political and economic lives. Given the widespread international phenomenon of citizen disillusionment with and distrust and distance from their political systems, it may be that the time is ripe for economic organizations, especially universities, to step into the moral gap created by corrupt or inefficient governments. This will depend on whether universities can find a transparent economic ethic which determines their business. For example, the creation of social inequalities as a by-product of output may not be an acceptable outcome of a defensible ethics of the firm or university.

The problem of identity remains. The concepts of world citizen, of basic human rights, do not yet seem strong enough to bear the force of the obligation to behave in any other way than self-interest. Lester Thurow (1992) has suggested that President Clinton has to establish a philosophical position on the nature and extent of personal altruism before an economic policy for the twenty-first century can be established. This issue is vital because the answer determines the extent and nature of government intervention needed to secure basic human needs for its deserving citizens. In Britain, low wages sustained by high mass unemployment and low corporate taxation have encouraged international companies to locate or expand. Yet the restricted taxable base, caused by low wages and unemployment and low corporate taxes, leads to an impotent state which lacks the public revenues (given national debt ceilings) to build a proper infrastructure. Unless corporations take on community responsibilities at the point of location, irrespective of the national origins of the company, citizens may be unduly impoverished by this policy and resources vacuum. The trend for British universities to establish operations in other countries is a case in point. Paradoxically, as Reich (1993) has claimed, there is a growing connection between the amount and kind of investment that the public sector undertakes and the capacity of a nation to attract world-wide capital. Corporations are attracted by convivial infrastructure (high quality welfare systems) but this may be lacking because of the nature of other equally important location and expansion factors – specifically, a low wage, low income, politically indifferent population.

Lipietz (1992) has argued that Fordism intensified under Reagan in the USA and Thatcher in Britain, yet the political and economic infrastructure which supported it has collapsed. The weakening of publicly secured welfare resources and of labour protection legislation and the deregulation (through the disappearance of nationally negotiated wage settlements) of labour markets has been seen to be replaced by the emergence of a new model citizen, the Hurd–Patten Active Citizen, as we have seen in Chapter 2. The problem, it seems, is not so much a lack of having but a lack of being. The vacuum created by the lack of national identity and the embryonic nature, at best, of corporate personal identity (except, it is claimed, in Japan) is to be filled by a re-creation of the self. The importance of altruism as part of the desired moral make-up of new post-Fordist citizens cannot be stressed too highly. Citizens, according to Lipietz (1992), want quality in consumption and will use their growing free time as the central focus for working out a new political economy of production and consumption. Altruism, an inclination or desire to have less so that others might have more of some valued good or service, might be seen through citizens being inclined to take their share of gains in productivity in free time rather than wages, and then to use their 'free time' in altruistic, philanthropic or charitable acts. Or they may choose to have less work for themselves so that unemployment can be reduced. University graduates have been known to rationalize their underemployment or unemployment or application for a postgraduate course by claiming a contribution to increasing the employment chances of others by taking themselves out of the labour market. Early retirement can be similarly justified if need be.

Lipietz's (1992) vision of a 'third sector' producing socially useful products with jobs for all at minimum agreed wages has been echoed in a vision of a sector that is neither market nor state. In any case, the usefulness of distinctions drawn by the division of state, private and voluntary sectors has long been questioned. In Britain the government has attempted to bring a traditionally conceived commercial ethic into the public services. Government itself is treated as a form of business. This movement creates considerable dislocations for producers and consumers since one of the old meanings of public sector has been that it offers services which no sane (profit maximizing) business would undertake yet which meet agreed human needs. The movement in Britain to make public services commercially accountable has been at the cost of losses in democratic accountability. Power is being transferred from democratic and representative institutions into the hands of what Professor John Stewart has called a 'new magistracy' of unaccountable managers (Bogdanor, 1993). This critique fails to recognize that this shift in accountability may not lead to an overall decline in morality. It depends on what sort of 'commercial ethic' is practised by the newly commercialized public systems. They will not need regulating, and Bogdanor's fear of lack of power of Parliament or local communities to control them will be unfounded, if their managers are internally regulated and policed by an appropriate business ethic. The University of Lancashire's social ethics audit of its internal management and organization is an example of an attempt to assess and subsequently change the morality of bureaucracy.

The internal policing of firms, whether public, private or 'third sector', could be facilitated by an active acceptance by firms of the force of the growth of Citizen's Charter movements (Audit Commission, 1993). In Britain, the government has been at pains to identify the best and worst councils in England and Wales. The Citizen's Charter introduced by Prime Minister John Major requires local government to answer 152 questions about their services. The findings from these questions were published in 1995 – local authorities were required to advertise the findings in newspapers. Some idea of the flavour of the move is given by the examples in Table 6.1.

Table 6.1 *Citizen's Charter – Examples of questions from the Audit Commission*

Service	Questions
Council-wide	How quickly does the council answer the telephone? Can the disabled get into public buildings easily?
Housing	How many squatters are there? How quickly are repairs carried out? How long do homeless people wait to be rehoused?
Environmental services	How good is the rubbish collection service? How easy is it to get to a rubbish dump? How are dogs controlled by the council?
Environmental health	How well does the council tackle the problem of noisy neighbours?
Education	How many children receive nursery education? How full are secondary schools? Can children eat hot meals at school?
Social services	Does the authority identify elderly people who need help in time? Are children (in care) looked after by people of similar ethnic culture?
Highways	Are the street lamps kept in working order? How quickly are potholes repaired?
Police	How many burglaries are solved by the police? How successful are the police in tackling drunken driving? How many complaints are made against the police?

The themes of identity and accountability within economic systems are exemplified by Care in the Community legislation in Britain. It is clear that this is failing in so far as people are suffering because Social Services Departments are arguing over who should pay for an individual's care if it is not clear to which county the person belongs. The Department of Health's own figures suggest that in the first three months of Care in the Community, local authorities, desperately juggling their budgets, reduced the number of placements funded in hostels providing residential and therapeutic care for alcoholics and drug dependants (Longsdale, 1993). Financially led Community Care is contrasted with the former needs-led system by many critics of Care in the Community legislation. Again, we have to say 'financially led' is not inevitably antagonistic to 'needs-led'. The crude transfer of a narrowly conceived caricature of private business practices to public service practices has yet again set up a conflict which need not exist.

John Smith, the former leader of the British Labour Party, in a speech to the Party's local government conference in Bournemouth in 1993, promised a 'new political approach for a new political era'. He claimed that the Labour Party in Britain offered a middle way between the 'equally discredited' planned economies of Eastern Europe and the free market ideologies of the USA:

> For years we have conducted a largely sterile debate about the ownership of industry and services as if privatisation and nationalisation were the only conceivable choices in economic policy.
>
> In the Labour Party we see the merits of a mixed economy and the need for an active and creative partnership between the public and private sectors. We also comprehend that in a world of multinational ownership of companies, the only true national asset we possess is the skills and accumulated knowledge of our own people. Ownership today is, therefore, largely irrelevant ... the ownership mania had moved from left to right.
>
> (Wintour, 1993)

We return to the claim of Lester Thurow, the great Nobel prize winning American economist, that the basis for any economic and political theory should be the resolution of disputes about human nature, specifically, the extent and nature of selfless acts. Starting from first principles, in this way, will enable some sense to be made of an emerging new welfare settlement which is characterized by decentralization, the strengthening of market forces, an autonomous managerialism, a stronger voice for consumers and an emphasis on value for money. What we are seeing is a coming together of organizations with prime social objectives, but increasingly important economic objectives, such as universities, with organizations with prime economic objectives, but increasingly important social objectives, such as reconstructed private firms. It is this pincer movement which is destroying the descriptive and analytical power of categorizing economic systems and organizations as primarily private, public, voluntary or NGO.

The question then arises, do we have a new economic order on our hands? The 'British Consumer "Lifestyles" survey' (Mintel, 1993) predicts the kinds of things the British will be spending money on in the next decade and the structural and social changes seen to change consumer demand (see Table 6.2). The findings suggest a defensive rather than caring and sharing society.

Table 6.2 *British Consumer Lifestyles Survey, 1993. Predicted changes in expenditure*

Growing Proportion of expenditure	%	Declining Proportion of expenditure	%
Insurance and pensions	+1.9	Food (in home)	−2.9
Medical and educational fees	+0.8	Home power (gas, electricity)	−1.2
Household services	+0.5	Clothing	−0.6
Household and garden products	+0.4	Tobacco	−0.5
Eating out	+0.4	Domestic appliances	−0.5
Entertainment	+0.4	Furniture and furnishings	−0.4

The impact on the individual of dispositions towards caring and sharing, as predicted by the Mintel 'Lifestyle' reports of the late 1980s, and the lived experience of impoverishment and anxiety, is the driving force behind personal economic behaviour. The latter appears to be winning. Does all this mean that we should be acknowledging that we have or will have a new economic order? Or does it mean that we should improve the economic system that we have? President Clinton knows that had the American economic system been perceived to be functioning in a reasonably satisfactory way under former President

Bush, he would not have been elected. In contrast, in Britain, the ability of the Labour Party to deny itself power, despite widespread public dismay about the comparative failings of the British economy under the Tories, is astonishing. Economics does matter, yet its influence seems unpredictable. Nonetheless, according to Professor J.K. Galbraith (1992) neither the USA nor the UK require a search for an alternative economic system:

> We are concerned with making more effective and more tolerant and equitable the economic system we have. Our claim is not to violent change, certainly not to revolution. It is to a socially better performance by the existing system.

How is this to be achieved? Galbraith, echoing Daniel Bell (1973), disputes the force of controlling principles – socialist, social democratic, liberal – and claims that ours 'is an age of constructive pragmatism'. Issues, he claims, must be decided on their merits and there must be 'no escape from thought into theology'. The economic problem to be resolved, as always, is one of scarcity and competition. What is socially intolerable and morally indefensible is the great and intolerable unequal distribution of income in the majority of countries. This, in a major way, is due to the world-wide economic tendency towards an underemployment equilibrium. The political task is to break societies out of this tendency since it is now clear that there are no 'natural' economic forces (at least in the short or medium term) that will do this. Lipietz (1992), as we have seen, anticipates people's preference for less work to be the basis of a policy for redressing economic inequality. Both Lipietz, from France, and Galbraith, from the USA, agree that societies, for basic business stability and macro-economic predictability, need a wage-negotiating process that is consistent with price stability. An acceptance of this by business and academic communities would be the signal for the emergence of a mature economic ethic. This will force the creation of an economic system that will see the planned convergence of aims which meet internal social need and more general economic policy. All agencies with economic objectives should work towards this wherever they find themselves in business and should be democratically accountable. Firms, including universities, should strive to be socially responsible in output and production process. Universities begin with prime social objectives, and have had to take on in a much more explicit and transparent way, a set of economic objectives. My point here is that they must be careful where they get their role model from for the adoption of higher profile economic objectives – not all industry is worth emulating, and be sure that they stay sure-footed in a slippery and dynamic world economy.

SOCIAL RESPONSIBILITY, THE FIRM AND THE UNIVERSITY

In order to describe how a firm or university should behave if it is to act in a socially responsible way, we need to identify and analyse the firm's incentives to be socially responsible. This in turn requires us to understand what a firm is and what governs the general behaviour of firms. Some key developments in the way economists have changed their understanding of the firm will be outlined and some implications suggested for predicting the conditions under which universities, as firms, might be expected to be socially responsible in their behaviour.

Richard Coase (1937), in an article which made him famous, raised the question: why do firms exist at all? At the most general level, where I do not intend to dwell, firms represent a response to the search, through democracy and capitalism, for the elimination of mass poverty and despotism, and for the establishment of efficiency and fairness in resource distributions. Mass poverty exists where a large number of the population lives at or near the minimum level of physical subsistence and despotism is found where the rulers are largely or entirely unaccountable to those being ruled (Bowles and Edwards, 1985). Efficiency is a position where no inputs are wasted. That is, for a given level of input, output is maximized or, to produce a given level of output, inputs are minimalized. Efficiency is best described as a waste preclusion theorem (Baumol, 1991). Fairness exists where, through due process, people are treated as equals and the outcomes of resource distribution are fair. That is, where there is general agreement that the winners, if there are any, deserve what they get and that the losers are properly looked after.

More specifically, economists have begun their analysis of the firm within democracy and capitalism by making two behavioural assumptions. First, firms are profit maximizers and second, people are utility maximizers. Firms are owned and controlled by individuals who maximize individual utility as well as seeking organizational profit maximization whilst, more generally, economic transactions are governed by the decisions of profit and utility maximizing producers and consumers.

These behavioural assumptions are the basis of classical General Equilibrium Theory, 'a major intellectual achievement' (Hahn, in Bell and Kristol, 1981). Classical GET is a theory of human behaviour since it describes a situation where private self-interest, governed only by market prices, can be consistent with a coherent and orderly economy. Hahn goes on to argue, however, that classical GET 'is likely to recede and be superseded', and we need to outline the basis of the new managerial theory of the firm to see where Hahn's prediction is being worked out.

No single objective (such as profit maximization) can fully lead to an accurate prediction of the firm's behaviour in a given market. Management strategy has been conceptualized as the 'programmatic choice among alternatives, none of which can prove satisfactory' (Hyman, in Scase, 1989). Profit maximization and utility maximization, in any case, are less plausible with the divorce of ownership from control in the modern firm and less plausible given the existence of altruists (Victor, 1972). Where ownership and control are separated, management sets the objectives. These can include an emphasis on achieving the highest value of sales revenue or the largest volume of production or the highest rate of growth of capacity. Each of these can lead to greater long-term security for the firm, to reductions in internal conflicts of interest and to less variability in profits, if not higher profits:

> The theories and concepts that govern the actual, as against the theoretical behaviour of firms are theories of the cost of capital, of market optimisation, and of the long range cost gain (the 'learning curve') from maximising productivity.
>
> (Drucker in Bell and Kristol, 1981, p. 14)

Peter Drucker, a guru of contemporary management economics, stresses the discrepancy between economic theory and the firm's behaviour. Yet economists have no real excuses for ignoring what firms claim to be for and testing these claims against performance. As firms become more public, access to their 'mission statements', 'corporate aims', 'codes of conduct' and so on means that at the least firms can be understood and evaluated on their own terms. For example, PepsiCo (1977) lists three 'fundamental objectives' for the Company, one of the world's largest (measured by sales and political and cultural influence):

- to earn the highest possible return on its shareholders investment consistent with fair and honest business practices
- to ensure steadily increasing per-share profits and dividends paid to shareholders
- to perform consistently better than the industry in every market where PepsiCo products and services compete

The next economics, Drucker has argued, in its macroeconomics, 'will, almost certainly, discard altogether the concept of profit' (in Bell and Kristol, 1981, pp. 13–14). Hahn, we have seen, argues that classical GET is likely to 'recede and be superseded' (in Bell and Kristol, 1981, p. 127). And we have established that firms are so complex that no single theory or single claim or objective, such as profit maximization, will do. Theory, indeed, is merging with practice.

> Management is differentiated into specialisms which supply their members with different conceptions of interest and world views, thus leading to differentiated views of and responses to the same external events.   (Salaman, in Scase 1989, p. 53)

Where, then, can the imperative of socially responsible behaviour and organizational structure fit in? This imperative to be virtuous, for firms and firm emulating organizations, for individuals and for governments, has climaxed in the late twentieth century for a variety of reasons. Suffice it to say that, generally, all firms in the 1990s can be best understood as representing a conflict between the economic goal of entrepreneurial activity and the forced accommodation of social objectives, all, in the UK, in the context of a political enthusiasm for enhanced competition between all organizations and individuals. This is the economic milieu universities inhabit.

Why 'forced'? A rational firm, unless social objectives are its prime purpose (and we have seen that a single set of objectives is unlikely to be the case), has no incentive to do anything which is not compatible with its economic objectives, whatever they are. Firms are economic organizations first and foremost. Where, then, is the incentive to be socially responsible to come from? This can only come from pressure derived from the preferences of individuals as economic units or, collectively, through governments.

> Only government action which forces good behaviour even upon managements that care little about such issues can permit more responsible business persons to undertake more than token acts toward environmental improvement in a perfectly contestable market ... A business person who really favours effective action to cure the environmental damage caused by the industry can contribute most effectively toward that goal not by attempts to institute a voluntary programme within her own firm, but by supporting well designed legislation. Such legislation will impose such behaviour upon the entire industry ... The notion that firms should by themselves pursue the objectives of society is, in fact, a rather frightening proposition. Corporate management holds in its hands enormous financial resources. Voluntarism suggests, or rather demands, that management uses these resources – other people's money – to influence the social and political course of events. But who is to determine in what way these events ought to be influenced? Who is to select these goals? If it is management itself, the power of interference with our lives and the lives of others that management is asked to assume is surely intolerable.   (Baumol, 1991, p. 43)

We know that large corporations can and do act as if they are governments. In which case it is appropriate, where accurate, to describe large corporations as despotic where they fail to act democratically or neglect to create an internal democracy. The notion that firms should by themselves be the major organizations which seek to realize the objectives of society is only tenable if firms are democratic institutions, open to control and open to adopting alternative agendas. If not, as Baumol has argued, it is a frightening proposition that the firm or university should be the major instrument for meeting the collective wishes or delivering the general will. The enormous financial resources and, hence, political power, of corporate management are a major influence on social change. But the power of interference in our political and social lives, as well as economic lives (of management), is potentially intolerable. All major agencies of social change – firms, governments, educational institutions, voluntary associations and families – have, in economic terms, to balance entrepreneurial activity with social objectives in a competitive climate. We need to work out some ground rules which establish socially responsible behaviour as the main evaluative criteria for judging the outcomes of these complex interactions as well as evaluating the nature of the interactions themselves. This is as true for universities as for any other organization with social and economic objectives.

What sort of game is this? Game theory can be helpful in conceptualizing the incentives to be socially responsible. Hirschleifer (1982) suggests a number of fruitful applications of game theory to understanding economic behaviour in adversity – under uncertainty. Imagine that a number of companies, all with subsidiary companies owned or controlled by themselves, are trading in a particular market, say property developers building for tourism development, or universities franchising their first year undergraduate social science programmes to Colleges of Further Education or to universities in other countries. The impact of these companies in terms of their type and level of socially responsible behaviour could be judged by the policy of the worst firms, or weakest link in the industry. If socially responsible behaviour is a public good, then we need a planning and development framework for higher education in the UK such that the activities of the worst university are sufficiently good to avoid irresponsible outcomes. Hirschleifer makes this point through offering the fantasy of a low lying country, surrounded by sea and threatened by flooding at abnormal high tides. Each plot of land on this more or less circular island is similar in size and shape, much like portions of a pie, with each plot at its narrowest at the centre of the island, and each having a border at the water's edge. The land is privately owned. The method of flood protection is to use dikes. If these are not built, or not built high enough or well enough, by any individual land owner, their plot will be flooded, and so will every other plot of land. In this case, the optimum height and quality of the dike for the individual is that which is just high enough and just strong enough to protect the land from the worst predicted flood. If each individual builds such a dike, they have inevitably, Hirschleifer says, voluntarily invested in a dike which provides both the private good and the public good of flood protection. This example easily and powerfully illuminates the recent history of higher education policy in the UK since it stresses the obligation facing all universities to see themselves not only as part of a competitive system but as part of a mutually supporting system, since the economic activities of the least socially responsible university potentially sets the political and cultural context for all the rest.

As Baumol has suggested we need 'well designed legislation ... to impose behaviour upon the entire industry'. But this may not be the best policy. Imagine, Hirschleifer suggests, a team marksmanship competition – archery or pistol shooting springs to mind. All members of the team want to achieve glory, a public good, but how is the winning team to be identified? At least three possibilities exist. The first possibility is that each score from each competitor in the team could be added together, the total score calculated and the team with the highest score determines the winner. The second possibility would be to judge the winning team as the team with the least worst total score by each of the team's members. That is, the best total score by the worst member of each team would determine the winning team. The third possibility would be to take the highest total score by the best competitor in each team. If we apply these three positions to the new global universities we can begin to make some claims about the appropriate targeting of legislation (Baumol, 1991), drawing on international law.

We have to say that the winning firm is the firm which achieves glory through establishing the highest level of socially responsible behaviour.

1. *Total score wins.* There, all of the subsidiary organizations, such as FE Colleges, as well as the main university, matter. They all need to be regulated since any one will detract from the possibility of achieving glory.
2. *Best score of the worst team member.* Here, the idea of a minimum standard of behaviour is the target for legislation with the additional focus on raising this minimal level of behaviour to its highest level. In preparation for the archery competition, the focus of training would be on raising the standard of the predicted worst performers. For the university, the behaviour of its most irresponsible component would need to be clearly within the effective influence of the regulatory framework. For universities in the franchise business, this raises questions about the respective legal and financial regulatory frameworks within each institution, as well as the nature of codes, charters and so on that might apply.
3. *Best score of the best team member.* This is clearly not acceptable as a criteria for judging the firm or university and its behaviour, but this may happen. One excellent Department in an overall lowly graded set of Departments may 'lift' the overall status of the university far above what the average quality level would suggest.

Its best activities could be easily offset by its worst activities. Yet, governments do invest in awarding prizes to the best firms. In Britain, there are the Queen's Awards to Industry, awards for the best industrial training programmes within firms, awards for productivity gains, and so on. These awards allow a company to put the imprimatur of the award on all its activities, including its subsidiaries, yet only one part of the firm may have invested in earning the award. If we now return to Hirschleifer's land and the anti-flooding policy, and use Baumol's analysis, we see that we should try to ensure that each university through self-interest or voluntarily invests in ensuring that its potentially most irresponsible behaviours are never bad enough to threaten the achievement of the public good of socially responsible higher education.

What do we know about how managers think and how does their thinking fit with the frameworks emerging from business ethics? Do academic managers think the same way as other managers? A recent survey of 60 managers (Ulrich and Thielman, 1993) using in-depth interviews, concluded that managers start their thinking with market conditions. More specifically, they try to best guess what the 'invisible' hand of market forces is likely to do to sales and then plan and implement strategies in order to turn these forces and predicted outcomes to the benefit of their companies. This interesting paradox, accepting the invisibility of forces yet focusing on intervening to control the influence of these forces, is not enough for an emerging breed of 'New Managers'. These have achieved an: 'integrative conceptualisation which links entrepreneurial success with ethical reasoning in a way that adequately addresses the societal problems of business today' (Ulrich and Theilman, 1993). So, we have the creation, it is claimed, of a new market morality which goes beyond the superficially convincing but global and unspecified social contract theories which have attracted some commentators, and which is more expansive than the popular professional and corporate codes which have specific but restricted validity, being limited to a group or named people. The work of university admission officers and the words in university prospectuses might be examined in this light.

THE SOCIALLY RESPONSIBLE UNIVERSITY

Can we then agree that some sort of 'integrative conceptualization' is needed to work rationally for the creation of the socially responsible university? What needs to be identified in order for 'entrepreneurial success' and 'ethical reasoning' to be more than mere words is a clear and pragmatic scheme that allows the members of a university (or those who have substantial rights of influence over its affairs) to create a model firm. Such a firm would be socially responsive to its influence over its social environment through its own activities, would have a social conscience in terms of its part in dominant social issues which it inherits (through geography and history) and which contextualizes its business, and would have workers and customers who are actively sensitive to their social obligations as worker–citizens and consumer–citizens. These three elements combine to allow the establishment of a corporate social policy (Harvey, 1992) which would be a balance of principles relating to: human rights, the specific moral claim of stakeholder groups, and to efficiency and productivity.

This university needs one more element in order to secure the accurate label of being socially responsible. It would have to recognize that the ultimate ethical test is what position it takes on human nature. This is the battle ground on which the integration of a theory of society and a theory of education has to be fought. No theory of education is acceptable which does not arise out of a theory of society and this theory has to spell out the sort of society which is preferred (Dewey, 1944; also see Chapter 1). Economic theory is useful here since, as we have seen, the classic duality of individual consumption maximization as the driving force behind individual behaviour, and profit maximization as the aim of economic organizations has been discredited and is beginning to be superseded. The primary focus of the university should be on its treatment of the people it is enabling to learn and on being able to defend its decisions on the selection of forms of knowledge it considers to be worthwhile developing and disseminating. Universities might wish to focus on enabling dissenting citizens to flourish (see Chapter 2).

Economists, when analysing human nature, now realize that they have to consider different economic 'types'. There may be a multitude of these, sometimes all to be found within one individual or, possibly existing as a single dominant trait within one individual for most of the time. Four different sets of characteristics are now well known: the self-maximizer, described as selfish and indifferent; the difference maximizer, who is quite happy to become worse off as long as other people become even worse off; the egalitarian, who does not mind what other people have as long as they do not have more than him; and the altruist, who actively strives to have less so that others can have more. These four types, or the traits they suggest, are found in many of us and clearly the willingness of the workers employed in universities and the chances of the consumers of higher education being socially responsible is significantly affected by the distribution of these characteristics in the population. Indeed, we can now argue that what might distinguish the prevalence of these 'types' is the distribution of the propensity to be socially responsible.

We can now also examine the confluence between the university as an organization and the motivations of the people who are the owners, workers and customers of the university. And here we can turn to orthodox political philosophy for help. We need an analysis of the concept of social responsibility at the level of the individual since the business of the university is essentially to do with the promotion of human welfare through offering learning infused with scholarship, and research directed towards the common good. Of major importance here is to tease out the meaning and significance of political obligation. Why should individuals not be self-interested as orthodox economics assume them to be? Is there some obligation acting on people which propels them beyond this, say, towards altruism?

The concept of social responsibility is usually treated in political philosophy as part of a discussion of obligation and political obligation in particular. Obligation has a number of interesting features. To begin with, there is a tension between the claim that obligation is a primary moral concept and the claim, from linguistic philosophy, that obligation suggests an unwilling acquiescence. So, if we are obliged to do something, we do it because it is the right thing to do: not to do it would be wrong (Raz, 1986). On the other hand, it is normally used in connection with some burdensome interpersonal behaviour of some social benefit. It is usual to identify three different types of obligation (with the accepted caveat of non-exclusivity):

• Social obligation: where an action is recognized by the consensus of public opinion or some relevant group of society.
• Legal obligation: something done which is valid in the courts of law.
• Political obligation: an outcome of some established political process.

Generally, our obligations are the sum of what is required of us as members of a society, a polity or a jurisdiction. They reflect our public lives. Obligations and interests need to be distinguished since, although they sometimes coincide, they are logically distinct. Obligations are not always in a person's interests. For example, we may be obliged to be honest but there are occasions when we want to lie. Obligations, however, are unconditional imperatives. They sit alongside trust as one of the building blocks of public life. Morality underwrites trust, as it does obligation, since without trust, there can be no social life. Trust is the basis of mutual reliance.

A linguistic approach to political theory would claim that the question 'Why should I obey the government?' is absurd. The person who asks it has not understood the concept of belonging. People who belong do not need justification for rules: if they belong to the club, they obey the rules. Obeying the rules is the defining character of membership and membership challenges individualism. The claim is sometimes made that humans are naturally social animals who only flourish in a social context. The state then can become, in modern times, the ultimate moral authority for securing the social conditions of individual freedom. The civil republican tradition in political thought claims that political life has intrinsic value – that is, our political obligations should not be burdensome. We often talk of the community's interest. A community defines a group of people who are not indifferent to one another's lot. The state, or national community, arises when the possibility is there for the state to come into being without being contrary to anybody's will. This happens when a voluntary agency transforms itself into the sole legitimate coercive protective association through securing:

- the voluntary adherence of the majority
- the coercion (potentially) of the minority without apparently infringing the minorities' rights

We can distinguish a community's internal interest, as, say, domestic peace and order and physical and mental health and its external interest as, generally, conditions favourable to achieving and maintaining the internal interests (for example, security from external attack; identifying economic markets where the community is not self sufficient). Normally, historically, the boundaries of internal and external are blurred (is the British Commonwealth 'external' to Britain?).

Socially responsible behaviour describes a situation where self interest is overridden by community interest whenever the two conflict (strong version), and whenever people act so as to always do what can be done to promote the community's interest (weak version). Social responsibility is part of public life and is not found in anarchy. It sustains communities not through the abandonment of self interest but through the pursuit of self interest in ways at least compatible with the community's interest. Difficulties arise, of course, when private interests within a community, say University Vice Chancellors' views on student funding, lay claims to being the public interest. Individuals belonging to a community are obliged to behave in a socially responsible way, that is, to obey the rules (although there are, as we shall see, exceptions). Put another way, communities have a corporate right to require their members to do whatever is necessary to maintain and promote the public interest. People who belong to a democratic political community are voluntary members – they could emigrate; and any individual cannot see beyond the complexity to visualize (accurately) what is the public interest and must, therefore, accept the legitimacy of claims to represent the public interest.

Political obligation can be understood as a specific form of the generic obligation to be socially responsible. The state or government has an obligation to act as a custodian of the public interest and the governed, or citizens, have an obligation to accept the government's legitimate authority in defining and working towards the public interest (subject to qualification – see below). This legitimate authority is a mixture of political and legal authority and is created through positive laws, especially constitutional law. Generally, this means a commitment to the Rule of Law where the supremacy of the law is acknowledged, which in turn secures the supreme authority of government, and where the principles of equality before the law and freedom under the law condition and sustain this supremacy. Communities dissolve (or fail to emerge) when the polarization of sectional interests lead to the absence of agreement about the basis of life in the wider (actual or potential) community. Polarization here shows the distance between the private and public interest and the distinct lack of possibility of social responsibility.

Anarchy has already been identified as not requiring any obligatory relationships or principles to sustain it. Political systems based on mutual reliance, trust, obligation and social responsibility do not rule out the legitimacy of civil disobedience or revolution where these are in the public interest. Indeed, one of the aims of illegitimate political action can be to reinvent these four sustaining moral concepts and to rescue them from what is claimed to be otherwise terminal decline. Civil disobedience, for example, as practised by British university students in the 1960s and 1970s, worked through its own orthodoxy characterized by, in a democratic society:

* being limited in scope
* being non violent (in intention)
* used as a last resort
* claiming to be just by appeal to moral principles

Revolutionary action takes in the third and fourth points above and is justified when reasonable prospects of success are present and the foreseeable consequences for maintaining public life (or the community) have been taken into account. The usual moral justification for the superiority of democracy over, say, a totalitarian state is that democracies recognize the autonomy of moral persons and recognize the role of reason in moral judgements. The coercion and restraint of (sane) moral persons needs to be justified to them if they are to feel a moral obligation to meet the public interest.

The term 'legitimation crisis' is a recent way of addressing the issue of obligation. Do universities in the UK face a legitimation crisis? We should always ask: do existing customs and conventions (social obligations) deserve our allegiance? Are they in the public interest? That these questions have been raised in an intense form recently, may be because of the perceived distance between the rhetoric and reality of the exercise of social responsibility. People may not be willing to quietly acquiesce within a community where their self interest is continually sacrificed to a public interest which sustains or thrives on gross inequalities. Universities might do well to remember this, for example, when scheming to dominate local rental housing markets. Jurgen Habermas (1988) in particular, has asked what acceptable *de jure* (the right to command and obey) political authority might look like. It would not include a community which undermines perfectly realizable human possibilities for flourishing, allows important human needs to be unmet, and permits identifiable human suffering. Herein lies the framework for the socially responsible university to influence its local (national and international, as appropriate) area of benefit for the good.

The people within such a community are individuals and collectively guilty of creating this legitimation crisis since the social 'bads' listed above are caused by an extensive, imposed consciousness which masks these bads or precludes their elimination. It is the psychological allegiance to humanity, coupled with the practical matter of survival, which allows, presumably, people such as Habermas to escape the bonds of their socialization and realize the truths of our existence. The problem of democracy in practice is that, for the underprivileged, choices are ignored and access to resources denied and this distortion, morally bad in itself, is compounded by being used to create and sustain privilege. Habermas claims that we need to establish non-ideologically bound legitimate beliefs which help us define the conditions which would really benefit our well-being and allow us to prioritize these distinctive human needs. A socially responsible university would play a key role in these processes.

> If potentially repressive institutions are rightly to be regarded as legitimate, it must be possible to imagine their creations under conditions of freedom and equality and their accep-

tance by the unforced consent of all those subsequently liable to be affected by their behaviours.   (Habermas, 1988, p. 51)

If there is no despotism of imposed consciousness, the state is a *de jure* and *de facto* (the means to enforce) legitimate authority and is owed unconditional obligation. In such a state (unlike totalitarianism) no-one could publicly reject morality and get away with it and all citizens would be morally equal – the life of everyone matters and matters equally. Furthermore, within this legitimate authority, trampling on the rights of the minority is no more justified if done by the majority than by another minority. Achieving such a society would be a necessary intention for any society, and any state which did not seek to achieve such conditions or which stood in the way of such potential progress would itself lose *de jure* legitimate authority and hence would not represent the public interest. Or, put another way, it would be blocking the achievement of social responsibility. Democracy in the 1990s, of course, is normally undermined, as Claus Offe (1984) has argued, by strong, class-based inequalities in the distribution of decision-making competence. The expansion of higher education in the UK in recent years may have, and certainly should have, ameliorated these inequalities and some universities, in their mission statements, have made a point of stressing their position on the relationship between access to higher education, future life chances for graduates and equality.

Terms such as 'the public interest', 'community' and 'mutual benefit' indicate that our actions usually impact on others. Obligations, we have seen, are often grudgingly acknowledged, but rights, which at the level of the individual are usually expressions of human needs, are stronger evocations of a demand for mutuality. Any genuine right must involve some normative direction of the behaviour of others (the relationship between obligation and duty is often blurred and may not be worth clearly distinguishing). Socially responsible behaviour is often argued for, given a high profile, by claiming rights to such behaviour. In our sense of obligation as a primary moral concept, people have rights, they might claim, to see out their obligations as any virtuous person would do. Interesting questions are whether such rights and their duty correlate or whether associated normative behaviour should transcend community boundaries?

Imagine two dissimilar countries. For example, if one of the countries is Islamic, where people do the will of God, there is no specific system of rights which locks together self interest and public interest. This problem of particularity can be overcome, as we have seen, by recourse to claims made about practical matters of survival and/or psychological allegiances to (common) humanity, or, more specifically, to a technical or emotional concept of global village or the community of one world. In any case, if visitors, including visiting academics, or students on exchange programmes, are allowed in, they must be tolerated; if visitors choose to go, they must be tolerant. What we need are some empirical studies of the limits of toleration. Universities might be interested in this.

According to Lord Scarman (1986) toleration has to exist on two fronts, a legal front and a social front, in order to guarantee a tolerant community. The law can and should define actions which we should repress because they do not deserve our toleration, and irrespective of the law, we should have values and attitudes which preclude toleration to certain behaviours. The main pragmatic (historical and linguistic) forms of toleration (and intolerance) have been sexual, racial, religious and political. Historically, toleration has meant to permit by law but not to endorse or encourage. Nonetheless, it is clearly the case that as well as 'live and let live', a toleration of diversity, there is a position which actively welcomes and celebrates differences. Within this theme of diversity sits uncomfortably, as we shall see, a form of dogmatism. For the justification of intolerance is through an appeal to the truth, the right way to behave. Toleration fuels the assertion that there is a correct way to live and nothing is to be gained by allowing people to live in a manner which is deeply misguided or morally wrong. Toleration, too, can be more than just about non-interference or leaving alone and can involve the acceptance or active support of the repression of wrong behaviour. This leads us, later, to discuss the paradox of toleration, an age-old problem whose resolution would go a little way towards providing a framework for the peaceful resolution of the disputes and protests by students, which, for example, are currently rocking South African universities.

Linguistically, we usually distinguish dislike from disapproval. Dislikes do not need toleration and only a few people would be expressing the same intensity of feeling when they say 'I do not think you should you wear Doc Martins with that formal ball gown' and 'I really disapprove of meat-eating'. There can, of course, be a fine line between the two but, like rights, it is easy to trivialize the concept of toleration if we attach it to matters of minor importance. The circumstances for toleration require (a) diversity and (b) that the nature of the diversity leads to disapproval or, more strongly, disgust.

The undesirable or the undesired are the prime candidates for both toleration and intolerance. Toleration is more than simply allowing something to exist (freedom to), to legally allow (licence by law), or to ignore (through indifference). If we speak of liberty or freedom to, there is no criticism implied. However, toleration means criticism since it has the property of disapproval or disgust. Otherwise, toleration is not needed. Moreover, to distinguish toleration from indifference, we need to add that the tolerant person must be in a position to influence behaviour. For example, we cannot be tolerant of someone getting too fat if this is linked to an incurable medical condition but we can be tolerant, if we choose, of someone who eats too much (where we disapprove of fatness). We are tolerant when we could successfully interfere with, influence or stop a behaviour but choose not to.

The ideological or intellectual roots of toleration, as Susan Mendus (1988) shows, are embedded in liberalism. In questions such as what is liberalism, what is its justification and what are its proper limits, the word 'liberalism' can be replaced by the word toleration. It is part of the liberal tradition since liberals often explain, describe, and defend their position as the arch promoters of liberty and toleration. Toleration may be a necessary condition for the promotion of freedom as well as being more than simply part of the circumstances of freedom. A pluralistic community requires toleration because it recognizes that not all values share its citizens' approval and that this disapproval cannot necessarily be reconciled harmoniously. This is why we need educational diversity in higher education in the UK within a defensible vision and practice of social responsibility. The source of much unhappiness in liberal states is caused by the need to be tolerant for those of us who find it distinctly uncomfortable allowing activities we disapprove of to continue. If all conflict could be eliminated with nothing of value lost then we would be in a single, utopian state where equality did not conflict with liberty, nor justice with mercy.

From the point of view of the individual, pluralism claims that no individual monopolizes all virtues. Indeed, some virtues may displace others (as do equality and liberty in the liberal state) because they are incompatible. It may be that creativity is incompatible with patience, yet both are virtues and value is lost if either is displaced or reduced. We tolerate the behaviour of others because we recognize that it is only perhaps because of the behaviours that we disapprove of that we have the virtues or good qualities. If the limitations did not exist, neither might the virtues. Within universities the need for toleration is often towards people or structures which govern our behaviour. Most frequently, proper thoughtfulness or sensitivity in some circumstances can seem like (and be) infuriating indecision, prevarication or plain fence sitting or deviousness, etc. The decision-making process needs to be transparent (Waldron, 1988). The workings and principles of the institution need to be well known and available for scrutiny. They should not be understood through mystification, mythology or the 'noble lie'. This, again, is a basic principle of liberalism. Within the liberal state, there should exist intelligible justifications in social and political life available to all, understood by the human mind, not justified by tradition, community, or need. The classic formulation of the liberal state is that it is open, diverse, plural and equally hospitable to all the beliefs of its members. In contrast the socialist, especially Marxist, state is closed, monolithic, uniform and treats diversity as deviance.

Toleration, as it is emerging in this analysis, is to do, at its weakest, with leaving others alone and certainly with refraining from persecuting them (unlike in totalitarian states). In this liberal state, where toleration will flourish as appropriate, toleration is limited by consideration of the truth. We need to decide whether people or their beliefs, practices or behaviour are morally wrong. If they are morally wrong, we can be reasonably intolerant. Where they are morally right and alterable and we disapprove, we need to be tolerant. Racial discrimination, for example, need not be tolerated (Ackerman, 1980). It is morally wrong to disapprove of qualities which are not freely chosen and unalterable. People are not responsible, as individuals, for the colour of their skin and cannot alter it. Racial discrimination is wrong and nothing (virtuous) is lost if it disappears. Why then should we ever tolerate that which we disapprove of, where we claim that someone or some action or belief is morally wrong? The claim of morally wrong can only be made if all rational people can agree with the claim – it has universal validity being the claim of a rational agent. One reason, as we have seen, is that if we get rid of some 'bads' we simultaneously get rid of the 'goods' (poverty – altruism). The strongest form of disapproval, where things become intolerable, leads to things being unbearable. Something which is unbearable is to be stopped and if not, much stress and strain may arise. But, we know that within liberalism, diversity must, at least, be accepted and, normally, celebrated. We need some mechanism for deciding whether intolerance is justified or not. Clearly, the socially responsible university would willingly grasp a role here for itself in promoting widespread informed public thought and discourse. If we can never be sure about what a moral truth or good is, if we remain sceptical, then in the liberal state, we err on the side of toleration. If there is nothing to chose between lifestyles, then there are no moral truths and, therefore, no one can presume to impose or rule. We then must allow different and, possibly, competing lifestyles. Within liberalism, of course, it is freedom and then equality that set the boundaries for this moral relativism so that lifestyles which deny or reduce either of these principles are deemed to be intolerable. These principles are a weak form of perfectionism, contrasted with a strong form such as fundamentalism.

If we are to let diversity flourish, are we to allow a belief that scepticism or neutrality is mistaken? It is a view, if left to flourish, which competes with all other views and may lead to their downfall. Someone may believe, fundamentally, that there is a way of life so morally superior that they feel morally obliged to impose it on others. This is a paradox of toleration, that is:

- The need for neutrality is created by the facts of diversity and scepticism.
- Can we be neutral about a view which denies the truth of the above statement?

The liberal state would not allow or sponsor the dominance of one concept of the good over another. The state and all members of it will remain sceptical and, therefore, neutral, about competing moral truths and will be tolerant of all of them. Each person within such a state is autonomous in the sense that each person is then able to live their life in their own way. Autonomy is logically derived from the toleration of diversity within a framework of moral truth. J.S. Mill (1978) argued that there is a truth about the best way to lead one's life but people should find their own way to that truth. The truth cannot be imposed. The state then functions as a way of satisfying the wants people have, not as a means to make people good. The state, according to Mill, should not exist to cultivate desirable wants or dispositions in its citizens. Notions of academic freedom and claims by university academics to be the guardians, along with other social mechanisms, of freedom of speech, need to be considered with due regard to the paradox of toleration, and to Mill's views on the limits of the state.

There is a problem here, of course, that post-modernism addresses. If I ask 'Am I free?' then I need to distinguish whether freedom is defined as satisfying the needs or desires I have, or whether it is about satisfying the desires I would have if I were more rational, better informed, self-willed, self-disciplined and less confined and /or manipulated? Autonomy is about rational self-determination, which is the pre-condition for human flourishing within the liberal state. The paradox of toleration, as earlier defined, is resolved here through only remaining neutral towards people's beliefs or actions which arise from rational self-determination. For example, a subculture of non-autonomous seeking individuals (based on religious fundamentalism) which withdraws from society to avoid contamination from it, who may establish their own university to propogate their beliefs, will not warrant neutrality from the state. (This is the beginnings of an argument for justifying the imposition by the agents of the state of blood transfusions on unwilling Jehovah's Witnesses.) The unity of diverse, plural, liberal societies and that which gives them their collective identity is that they all subscribe, within their separate solidarities, to the application of rational self-determination. Solidarities or collectives which refute this are not part of the university. They are not sceptical and their lack of scepticism denies the scepticism of others and precludes neutrality. This is a limit of toleration.

Toleration is needed to enable people to find their own way to the truth, as long as, in liberal societies, this truth arises from autonomous, rational, self-determining individuals. Liberal societies are less tolerant than their advocates would have us believe. The scope of neutrality is set by the sorts of things neutralists are neutral between and the application of government policies that are neutral is limited by the possibility of finding such policies. Governments and universities might be neutral by supporting rock and roll and opera; they should not be neutral between arsonists and non-arsonists.

J.S. Mill (1978) argued that the sole warrant for government interference was to prevent or remove harmful behaviour. This sounds appealing but there are well-known problems here. Do we stress physical harm, or moral harm to character, or harm to institutions, ways and forms of life (animals) or serious offence to feelings? Or all of these, including the negative perspectives of failing to benefit someone, and failing to meet a public obligation? Our answers to these questions tell us how wide, how value laden and, hence, how controversial the scope of government is to be, and how far universities should attempt to prescribe the behaviour of their students.

Earlier, we defined toleration as being required when we disapprove. However, we have now limited the extent of toleration to those things we disapprove of but do not cause some identifiable form of harm. Harm here would mean something which denied autonomy in people. The Williams Report (1979) is a classic example of an otherwise distinguished report which failed to defend the use of the harm principle. It showed that the concept of moral harm, when derived from consideration of obscenity and censorship, would lead to endless interference by and almost unlimited legislative powers for the state. Andrea Dworkin (1981) has argued, though, that pornography is not wrong because of the consequences (the line Williams took) but because it is wrong in itself since it is harmful in itself. The very existence of the activity is an offence and causes harm. If we accept this and follow Mill (1978) we can legitimate state interference since the only all-embracing principle is to delineate that which is harmful and prevent or remove it. This still leaves disagreement about the identification of harm and the paradox of toleration becomes apparent again ('one man's beef is another man's BSE').

Indeed, neutrality in outcome may be impossible. Susan Mendus (1989) gives the example of Sunday Trading laws in the UK. When these are introduced, they favour the Christians over the atheists and, if not, vice versa. As we have seen, we can only accept practical outcomes which do not do harm to some valid conception of the good life (such as autonomous individuality). Ronald Dworkin's (1985) concept of the good life, alternatively, focuses on equal concern and respect for all. That is, there would be no laws which favour one concept of the good rather than any other and all laws must be transparently justifiable in supporting equal concern and respect for people as human beings. For Dworkin, the only inequalities would be deserved inequalities, resulting from choosing to be unequal (smokers who die earlier rather than later). The concept of equality is contentious, as we would expect. How can a liberal society ensure that there is either: an equal flourishing of all conceptions of the good; or all have an equal chance; or all actually equally flourish?

In any case, where inequalities are the result of free choice rather than something suffered, there is no justification for state action. Neutrality requires adjustments to accommodate needs which are suffered, not preferences which are chosen. Where inequality is undeserved, equal treatment by the state is not required. However, if we take, for example, a person with physical disabilities applying to university it is not clear whether additional state resources are deserved because the handicap is not chosen (assuming it is inherited) or because the handicap deserves compensation or because the handicap gets in the way of the personal realization of needs. A hard case concerns 'voluntary' disabilities (for example, where people injure themselves through sporting activities).

People must be tolerant to others whose loyalty to a sub culture may conflict with their loyalty to the state. The test of rational self-determination can still hold since people can only truly belong on terms acceptable to them – community cannot be imposed. Similarly, the recipients of toleration (within liberalism too) can feel alienated by its practical outcomes (for example, telethons). People want respect, esteem and inclusion, not toleration. We have already seen the problem, more prevalent in socialist states perhaps, where racial and sexual tolerance is widespread and directly contradicts the ideological orthodoxy. For toleration, as we have seen, asserts something to be morally reprehensible and alterable. The limit to toleration within socialism is a desire to secure a sense of belonging for all. We need toleration not, as in liberalism, because we are all separate free agents but because we are all (potentially) interdependent victims.

THE UNIVERSITY, SOCIAL JUSTICE AND SPATIAL SYSTEMS

What role can the socially responsible university play in this? People who work in universities as academics and administrators are, by and large, privileged compared to the majority of people who live within the local area of benefit of the university. A justification for this privilege would be if the university was clearly seen to be active in forming alliances, partnerships, associations and other forms of power-sharing relationships with significant local groups and organizations who deserve to flourish as well as targeting the needs of the worse-off members of the locality (where the privilege may be starkest). In order to be selective in its external relations, the university needs to establish a clear ethical framework which directly informs policy and practice. Also, the internal affairs, procedures and other bureaucratic frameworks must be capable of acting as role models for local institutions in terms of the quality of treatment of employees and clients. The university then educates through being. A socially responsible university would seek a just distribution justly achieved (Harvey, 1973). Harvey, in his brilliant book, *Social Justice and the City*, was suitably humble about the contribution academics had made at that time to understanding the meaning and influence of the city:

> It took many years and an incredible application of intellectual resources to get to even a satisfactory beginning point for specifying a location theory based on efficiency and there is still no general theory of location – indeed we do not even know what it means to say that we are 'maximising the spatial organisation of the city' for there is no way to maximise on the multiplicity of objectives contained in potential city forms.   (p. 48)

We can substitute the word 'university' for 'city' since many universities, in relation to their locality, are the city within a city (in urban areas) and, in largely rural areas, the university is the city. The academic analysis of the meaning and significance of the university and what this should be needs to use the work of Morgan and Harvey together with insights from managerial economics, business ethics and political philosophy, as sketched in this chapter, in order to rationally and morally justify planned interventions in people's lives. The scope of influence of the modern university is vast. Universities, as modern economic corporations, need to work out the contradictions, and the subsequent risk and uncertainty which arises from these contradictions, between democracy and efficiency in the full public glare of sceptical individuals in order to secure long-term, sustainable survival.

REFERENCES

Ackerman, B.A. (1980) *Social Justice in the Liberal State*. New Haven: Yale University Press.
Allen, G. and Martin, I. (eds) (1992) *Education and Community: The Politics of Practice*. London: Cassell.
Aronowitz, S. and Giroux, H. (1985) *Education Under Siege*. London: Routledge and Kegan Paul.
Audit Commission (1993) *The Citizen's Charter Performance Indicators*. London: HMSO.
Baumol, W. (1991) *Private Markets and Easy Virtue*. Oxford: Blackwell.
Bell, D. (1973) *The End of Ideology*. New York: Basic Books.
Bell, D. and Kristol, I. (1981) *The Crisis in Economic Theory*. New York: Basic Books.
Bogdanor, V. (1993) 'When the buck doesn't stop here anymore'. *Observer*, 20 May.
Bowles, S. and Edwards, R. (1985) *Understanding Capitalism*. New York: Harper Row.
Brummer, A. (1993) 'New culture at large in the boardroom'. *Guardian*, 26 February.
Coase, R. (1937) 'The Nature of the firm'. *Economica*, **4**, 386–405.
Dewey, J. (1966) *Democracy and Education*. New York: Free Press.
Dworkin, A. (1981) *Pornography: Men Possessing Women*. New York: Woman's Press.
Dworkin, R. (1985) *A Matter of Principle*. Cambridge, MA: Harvard University Press.
Galbraith, J. (1992) *Lecture to the Institute of Public Policy*. London.
Gamble, A. (1986) *Britain in Decline*. London: Macmillan.
Habermas, J. (1988) *The Philosophical Discourse of Modernity*. Cambridge: Polity.
Harris, P. (1990) *On Political Obligation*. London: Routledge.
Harvey, B. (1992) *Times Higher Education Supplement*, 11 November.
Harvey, D. (1973) *Social Justice and the City*. London: Edward Arnold.
Hirschleifer, F. (1987) *Economic Behaviour in Adversity*. Brighton: Wheatsheaf.
Kane, F. (1993) 'Curse of the Company'. *Guardian*, 21 January.
Lipietz, A. (1992) *Towards a New Economic Order*. Cambridge: Polity.
Locke, J. (1983) *A Letter Concerning Toleration*. New York: Hackett.
Longsdale, S. (1993) 'The Stand Up for Yourself Society'. *Observer*, 4 July.
Mendus, S. (1988) *Justifying Toleration: Conceptual and Historical Perspectives*. Cambridge: Cambridge University Press.
Mendus, S. (1989) *Toleration and the Limits of Liberalism*. London: Macmillan.
Mill, J.S. (1978) *On liberty*. London: Penguin.
Mintel (1993) *The British Consumer*. London.
Morgan, G. (1986) *Images of Organisations*. Beverly Hills: Sage.
Offe, C. (1984) *Contradiction of the Welfare State*. London: Hutchinson.
PepsiCo (1977) *PepsiCo Incorporated Annual Report*. New York.
Raz, J. (1986) *The Morality of Freedom*. Oxford: Clarendon.
Reich, R. (1993) *The Work of Nations*. New York: Simon & Schuster.
Scarman, L. (1986) *The Scarman Report*. London: Penguin.
Scase, A. (1989) *Industrial Societies*. London: Unwin.
Smith, J. (1993) *Labour Party Local Government Conference*. Bournemouth.
Thurow, L. (1992) *Head to Head*. New York: Morrow.
Ulrich, P. and Theilman, V. (1993) 'Ethics and economic success'. *Journal of Business Ethics*, **12**(11), 879–98.
Victor, P. (1972) *The Economics of Pollution*. London: Macmillan.
Waldron, J. (1988) 'Locke, toleration and the rationality of persecution'. In Mendus, S. *Toleration and the Limits of Liberalism*. London: Macmillan.
Williams, B. (1979) *Report of the Committee on Obscenity and Film Censorship* (The Williams Report). London: HMSO.
Wintour, P. (1993) 'Smith sees Labour as the party of ambition'. *Guardian*, 22 March.

Bibliography

Aarrons, M. and Gittens, T. (1992a) *The Handbook of Autism – A Guide for Parents & Professionals*. London: Routledge.

Aarrons, M. and Gittens, T. (1992b) *The Autistic Continuum. An Assessment & Intervention Schedule*. London: NFER Nelson.

Acherson, N. (1988) *Observer*, 10 October.

Ackerman, B.A. (1980) *Social Justice in the Liberal State*. New Haven: Yale University Press.

African National Congress (1988) *In-house Seminar*. July, Johannesburg.

African National Congress (1991) *Press Statement on Violence*. 27 April, Johannesburg.

African National Congress (1993a) *Negotiations Bulletin, No. 32*. 8 July, Johannesburg.

African National Congress (1993b) *National Land Commission, Land Update*, Johannesburg.

Ager, L. (1993) *Psychological Coping Strategies in Mozambican Refugees*. Paper to the III European Congress on Psychology, Tampere, Finland.

Allen, G. (1979) 'Researching political education in schools and colleges', *International Journal of Political Education*, 2(1), 67–82.

Allen, G. *et al.* (1987) *Community Education: An Agenda for Educational Reform*. Milton Keynes: Open University Press.

Allen, G. and Martin, I. (eds) (1992) *Education and Community: The Politics of Practice*. London: Cassell.

Amnesty International (1992) *Torture, Ill-treatment and Executions in ANC Camps*. Johannesburg, December.

Andrews, C. (1992) 'Development of thought'. In Arendt, L. *Living & Working with Autism*. London: The National Autistic Society.

Arbuthnot, F. (1994) 'Iraq's innocents suffer the loss of childhood'. *Guardian*, 31 December.

Aronowitz, S. and Giroux, H. (1985) *Education under Siege*. London: Routledge and Kegan Paul.

Audit Commission (1993) *The Citizen's Charter Performance Indicators*. London: HMSO.

Ball, S. (1981) *Beachside Comprehensive*. Cambridge: Cambridge University Press.

Baron, S. *et al.* (eds) (1981) *Unpopular Education*. London: Hutchinson.

Baron-Cohen, S. (1987) 'Autism and Symbolic play'. *British Journal of Developmental Psychology*, 5, 139–48.

Bastiani, J. (1987) 'Professional versus lay authority'. In Allen, G. *et al.*, *Community Education: An Agenda for Educational Reform*. Milton Keynes: Open University Press.

Baumol, W. (1991) *Perfect Markets and Easy Virtue*. Oxford: Blackwell.

Bell, D. (1973) *The End of Ideology*. New York: Basic Books.

Bell, D. and Kristol, I. (1981) *The Crisis in Economic Theory*. New York: Basic Books.

Blaug, M. (1971) *An Introduction to the Economics of Education*. London: Allen Lane.

Bogdanor, V. (1993) 'When the buck doesn't stop here anymore'. *Observer*, 20 May.

Bonnerjea, L. (1994) *Family Training: A Good Practice Guide*. London: SCF.

Boothby, N. (1989) *Helping Traumatised Children: A Training Manual for a Treatment and Family Unification Program*. Maputo: SCF.

Boothby, N. *et al.* (1988) *Children of Mozambique: The Cost of Survival*. New York: USCR.

Bowles, S. and Edwards, R. (1985) *Understanding Capitalism*. New York: Harper Row.

Brennan, T. (1981) *Political Education in a Democracy*. Cambridge: Cambridge University Press.

Broadfoot, P. (ed.) (1984) *Selection, Certification and Control*. Brighton: Falmer Press.

Brown, R.D. *et al.* (1986) 'Stress on campus: an interactional perspective'. *Research in Higher Education*, **24**(1), 97–112.

Brown, W. (1992) 'Positive intervention'. In Module 2, Unit 4 of Autism Distance Learning Programme, The University of Birmingham.

Brown, W. (1993) 'What is a good school for this child?' In Collection of Papers from Study Weekend on Asperger's Syndrome. London: Inge Wakehurst Trust.

Brummer, A. (1993) 'New culture at large in the boardroom'. *Guardian*, 26 February.

Calvo, L. (1993) *Overview of the Evaluation of Community Based Psycho Social Therapy Programmes for Children in Situations of Armed Conflict*. New York: UNICEF.

Chanan, G. and Gilchrist, L. (1974) *What School is For*. London: Methuen.

Charnley, H. and Langa, J. (1992) *Social Welfare Interventions for Unaccompanied Children in Mozambique*. Maputo: SCF.

Chimienti, G. and Abu Nasr, J. (1992) 'Children's reactions to war-related stress II'. *International Journal of Mental Health*, **21**(4) (Winter 92/93), 72–86.

Christie, P. and Hall, B. (1993) *Parents as Partners*. Autism Module, Autism Distance Learning Programme, University of Birmingham.

Christie, P. and Wimpory, D. (1986) 'Recent research into the development of communicative competence and its implications for the teaching of autistic children'. *Communication*, **20**(1), 4–7.

Coase, R. (1937) 'The Nature of the firm'. *Economica*, **4**, 386–405.

Connelly, M. (1990) 'Foreword'. In Jordan, R. and Powell, S. *The Special Curricular Needs of Autistic Children: Learning and Thinking Skills*. London: The Association of Head Teachers of Autistic Children and Adults.

Crick, B. (1975) 'Basic Concepts'. Document 3 of the Programme for Political Education. In Crick, B. and Porter, A. (1978) *Political Education and Political Literacy*. London: Longman.

Crick, B. and Lister, I. (1974) 'Political literacy. The centrality of the concept'. In Crick, B. and Porter, A. (1978) *Political Education and Political Literacy*. London: Longman.

Cummings, C.E. (1971) *Studies in Education Costs*. Edinburgh: Scottish Academic Press.

Curran, P. (1988) 'Psychiatric aspects of terrorist violence. Northern Ireland, 1969-1987'. *British Journal of Psychiatry*, **153** (October), 470–5.

Danieli, Y. (1985) 'The treatment and prevention of long term effects and intergenerational transmissions of victimisation'. In Figley, C.R. *Trauma and Its Wake*. New York: Brunner-Mazel.

Danieli, Y. (1993a) In Williams, M.B. and Somer, W. *Handbook of Post Traumatic Therapy*. New York: Praeger.

Danieli, Y. (1993b) *Group Project for Holocaust Survivors and Their Children*. New York: UNICEF.

Daniels, H. and Ware, J. (1990) *Special Education Needs in the National Curriculum: The Impact of the E.R.A.,* The Bedford Way Series, University of London.

Dawes, A. (1990) 'The effects of political violence on children'. *International Journal of Psychiatry*, **25**, 13–31.

Dearing, R. (1993) In Jenkins, S. 'The Dearing Review'. *Devon Education News*.

Department of Education and Science (1978) *Special Educational Needs* (The Warnock Report). Report of the Committee of Enquiry into the Education of Handicapped Children and Young People. London: HMSO.

Department of Education and Science (1989) *Discipline in Schools* (The Elton Report). London: HMSO.

Desjarlais, R. (1993) *Political Violence and Mental Health*. A Review Paper prepared for the Harvard Project on International Mental and Behavioural Health. Cambridge, MA: Harvard University Press.

Dewey, J. (1944) *Democracy and Education*. New York: Free Press.

Dewey, J. (1956) *The School and Society*. Chicago: University of Chicago Press.
Dolan, C. and de Beer, M. (1994) *From Problems to Solutions*. Discussion document, ANC Education Workshop, Johannesburg, July.
du Toit, A. (1993) *Understanding South African Political Violence: a New Problematic?* New York: United Nations Research Institute for Social Development.
Dunnette, M.D., Motowidio, G.J. and Carter, G.W. (1990) 'An alternative selection procedure: the low-fidelity simulation'. *Journal of Applied Psychology*, **75**(6), 620–47.
Dworkin, A. (1981) *Pornography: Men Possessing Women*. New York: Woman's Press.
Dworkin, R. (1985) *A Matter of Principle*. Cambridge, MA: Harvard University Press.
Elbedour, S. *et al.* (1993) 'Children at risk: psychological coping with war and conflict in the Middle East'. *International Journal of Mental Health*, **2**(3) (Fall), 33–52.
Euromonitor (1990) *Young Britain: A Survey of Youth Culture in Transition*. London.
Feldman, K.A. (1976) 'Grades and college students' evaluations of their course and teachers'. *Research in Higher Education*, **4**(1), 69–111.
Fields, R. (1975) 'Psychological genocide: the children of Northern Ireland'. *Journal of Psycho-History*, **3**(2), 201–24.
Fisher, S. (1994) *Stress in Academic Life*. Milton Keynes: Open University Press.
Flanagan, J.C. (1954) 'The critical incident technique'. *Psychological Bulletin*, **51**(4), 327–58.
Free the Children Alliance, Johannesburg (1987) *Children and Detention*.
Frith, U. (1989) *Autism: Explaining the Enigma*. Oxford: Basil Blackwell.
Galbraith, J. (1992) *Lecture to the Institute of Public Policy*. London.
Gamble, A. (1986) *Britain in Decline*. London: Macmillan.
Garbarino, J. and Stott, F.M. (1990) *What Children Can Tell Us*. New York: Jossey Bass.
Gmelch, W.H. *et al.* (1984) 'Sources of stress in academe: a national perspective'. *Research in Higher Education*, **20**(4), 477–90.
Goldenberg, D. and Waddell, J. (1990) 'Occupational stress and coping strategies among female baccalaureate nursing faculty'. *Journal of Advanced Nursing*, **15**, 531–43.
Goldfarb, R.S. (1994) 'Dealing with arguably legitimate exam gripes: a possible Pareto improvement'. *Economic Inquiry*, **32**, 178–9.
Grandin, T. and Scariano, M. (1986) *Emergence Labelled Autistic*. Tunbridge Wells: Costello.
Green, A. and Sharpe, R. (1975) *Education and Social Control*. London: Routledge and Kegan Paul.
Habermas, J. (1988) *The Philosophical Discourse of Modernity*. Cambridge: Polity.
Hall, S. and Jefferson, T. (eds) (1976) *Resistance Through Rituals*. London: Hutchinson.
Hansard (1989) H.C. Deb, 4 December 1989.
Harris, P. (1990) *On Political Obligation*. London: Routledge.
Harvey, B. (1992) *Times Higher Education Supplement*, 11 November.
Harvey, D. (1973) *Social Justice and the City*. London: Edward Arnold.
Hirschleifer, F. (1987) *Economic Behaviour in Adversity*. Brighton: Wheatsheaf.
HMI (1979) *Aspects of Secondary Education in England*. London: HMSO.
Husen, T. (1979) *The School in Question*. Oxford: Oxford University Press.
Illich, I. (1969) *Deschooling Society*. London: Penguin.
Inglis, F. (1985) *The Management of Ignorance*. London: Basil Blackwell.
Jablensky, M.D. *et al.* (1991) *Stress Research Reports No. 229*. The First International Conference on the Mental Health and Well-being of the World's Refugees and Displaced Persons. Stockholm.
Jareg, E. (1993) *Rehabilitation of Child Soldiers in Mozambique*. Maputo: Redd Barna.
Johnson, P. and Martin, D. (1988) *Victims of Apartheid: Refugees, Returnees and Displaced Persons in Southern Africa*. Paper presented at the Oslo Conference on the Plight of Refugees, Returnees and Displaced Persons in Southern Africa.
Jolliffe, T., Lansdown, R. and Robinson, R. (1992) *Autism: A Personal Account*. London: National Autism Society.
Jones, G. and Meldrum, E. (1993) *Preliminary Findings and Implications for Practice Arising from an evaluative and Comparative Study of Current Interventions of children with Autism*. London: Department of Health and Department for Education.
Jordan, R. (1990a) *The National Curriculum: Access for Pupils with Autism*. London: Inge Wakehurst Trust.

Jordan, R. (1990b) 'Personal and Social Education and the Pupil with Autism'. In Collection of Papers from Study Weekend. London: Inge Wakehurst Trust.

Jordan, R. and Powell, S. (1990) *The Special Curricular Needs of Autistic Children: Learning and Thinking Skills*. London: The Association of Head Teachers of Autistic Children and Adults.

Kahn, R.L. *et al.* (1964) *Organizational Stress: Studies in Role Conflict and Ambiguity*. Chichester: J. Wiley.

Kane, F. (1993) 'Curse of the Company'. *Guardian*, 21 January.

Kanji, N. (1990) 'War and children in Mozambique: Is international aid strengthening or eroding community-based policies?'. *Community Development Journal*, **25**(2), 102–12.

Kellner, P. (1988) *Independent,* 17 October.

Lawyer's Committee for Human Rights (1986) *The War Against Children: South Africa's Youngest Victims*. December. Washington.

Lewis, A. (1991) *Primary Special Needs and the National Curriculum*. London: Routledge.

Lipietz, A. (1992) *Towards a New Economic Order*. Cambridge: Polity Press.

Lister, I. (1974) *Deschooling: A Reader*. Cambridge: Cambridge University Press.

Locke, J. (1983) *A Letter Concerning Toleration*. New York: Hackett.

Longsdale, S. (1993) 'The stand up for yourself society'. *Observer*, 4 July.

Lovaas, O.I., Caloun, K. and Jada, J. (1989) 'The nature of behavioural treatment and research with young autistic persons'. In Gilberg, R. (ed.) *Diagnosis and Treatment of Autism*. New York: Plenum.

Lowman, R.L. and Williams, R.E. (1987) 'Validity of self-ratings of abilities and competencies'. *Journal of Vocational Behaviour*, **31**, 1–13.

Macksoud, M. (1993) *Helping Children Cope with the Stresses of War*. New York: UNICEF.

MaClachlan, M. and McAucliffe, E. (1993) 'Critical incidents for psychology students in a refugee camp: implications for counselling'. *Counselling Psychology Quarterly*, **6**(1), 3–11.

Majodina, Z. (1989) *Factors Affecting Coping Modes Among South African Exiled Children*. Paper presented to the International Congress on Civil Rights, 16–18 June, Haikko, Finland.

McCain, R.A. (1990) 'Impulse-Filtering: a new model of freely willed economic choice'. *Review of Social Economy*, **48**, 125–43.

McCallin, M. and Fozzard, S. (1990) *Impact of Traumatic Events on the Psychological Well-being of Mozambican Refugee Women and Children*. Maputo: International Catholic Child Bureau.

McGuire, W.J. (1966) 'The current status of cognitive consistency theories'. In Feldman, S. (ed.) *Cognitive Consistency: Motivational Antecedents and Behavioral Consequents*. London: Academic Press.

McWhirter, C. *et al.* (1983) 'Belfast children's awareness of violent death'. *British Journal of Social Psychology*, **22**(11), 81–92.

Mendus, S. (1988) *Justifying Toleration: Conceptual & Historical Perspectives*. Cambridge: Cambridge University Press.

Mendus, S. (1989) *Toleration and the Limits of Liberalism*. London: Macmillan.

Mill, J.S. (1978) *On Liberty*. London: Penguin.

Miller, C. (1990) *Mozambique Family Tracing and Unification Programme*. London: SCF.

Mintel (1993) *The British Consumer*. London.

Morgan, G. (1986) *Images of Organisations*. Beverly Hills: Sage.

Mozambique National Directorate for Social Welfare (1985) *National Seminar on Children in Difficult Circumstances*. Maputo: Mozambique Ministry of Health.

Mozambique National Directorate for Social Welfare (1987) *Programme in Support of Children in Difficult Circumstances, 1985–1986*. Maputo: Mozambique Ministry of Health.

Munir, A.B.B. (1993) 'Child protection: principles and applications'. *Child Abuse Review*, **2**(2) (June).

Nader, K.O. *et al.* (1993) 'A preliminary study of Post Traumatic Stress Disorder and grief among the children of Kuwait following the Gulf Crisis'. *British Journal of Clinical Psychology*, **32**(4) (November), 407–16.

National Autistic Society (1993) *Approaches to Autism*. London.

NCC (1993a) *English in the National Curriculum*. York.

NCC (1993b) *Mathematics in the National Curriculum*. York.

NCC (1993c) *Modern Foreign Languages*. York.

Nozick, R. (1974) *Anarchy, State and Utopia*. Oxford: Basil Blackwell.

Offe, C. (1984) *Contradiction of the Welfare State*. London: Hutchinson.

OFSTED (1992) *Curriculum Organisation and Classroom Practice in Primary Schools*. London: HMSO.

Osipow, S.H. and Davis, A.S. (1988) 'The relationship of coping resources to occupational stress and strain'. *Journal of Vocational Behaviour*, **32**, 1–15.

Osipow, S.H. and Spokane, A.R. (1984) 'Measuring occupational stress, strain and coping'. In Oskamp, S. (ed.) *Applied Social Psychology Annual*. Vol. 5. Beverly Hills: Sage.

Pambookian, H.S. (1976) 'Discrepancy between instructor and student evaluations of instruction: effect on instructor'. *Instructional Science*, **5**, 63–75.

Pateman, C. (1970) *Participation & Democratic Theory*. Cambridge: Cambridge University Press.

Peacey, N. (1993) *Helping Children with Oral Communication Difficulties – A Team Approach*. Talk given at the College of St Mark and St John, Plymouth.

PepsiCo (1977) *PepsiCo Incorporated Annual Report*. New York.

Perkins, D., Guerin, D. and Schleh, J. (1990) 'Effects of grading standard information, assigned grade, and grade discrepancies on students' evaluations'. *Psychological Reports*, **66**, 635–42.

Pring, R (1984) *Personal and Social Education in the Curriculum*. London: Hodder and Stoughton.

Protacio-Marcelino, E. (1993) *Types of Psycho Social Programmes for Children in Armed Conflict*. New York: UNICEF.

Psychologist Journal (1992) *Psychological Research in Northern Ireland* (special issue).

Pynoos, R.S. (ed.) (1985) *Post Traumatic Stress Disorders in Children*. London: SCF.

Raundalen, M. *et al*. (1990) *Reaching the Children Through the Teachers. Helping the War Traumatised Child. A Manual*. Geneva: International Red Cross.

Rawls, J. (1972) *A Theory of Justice*. Oxford: Oxford University Press.

Raz, J. (1986) *The Morality of Freedom*. Oxford: Clarendon.

Red Cross (1993) *Guidelines for the Development of a Psychological Support Programme for Victims of Disasters and Other Stressful Life Events*. Geneva: International Red Cross.

Reich, R. (1993) *The Work of Nations*. New York: Simon & Schuster.

Ressler, E. *et al*. (1988) *Unaccompanied Children. Care and Protection in Wars, Natural Disasters and Refugee Movements*. Oxford: Oxford University Press.

Ressler, E. *et al*. (1993) *Children in War. A Guide to the Provision of Services*. Geneva: UNICEF.

Richard, G.V. and Krieshok, T.S. (1989) 'Occupational stress, strain and coping in university faculty'. *Journal of Vocational Behaviour*, **34**, 117–32.

Richman, N. (1988) *Psychological Effects of War on Children*. London: SCF.

Richman, N. (1991) *Reconciliation, Revenge? The Legacies of War*. London: SCF.

Richman, N. (1992) *Helping Children in Difficult Circumstances*. London: SCF.

Richman, N. (1993) 'Annotation: Children in situations of political violence'. *Child Psychology and Psychiatry*, **34**(8), 1286–302.

Roper, K. and Dawes, A. (1992) *The Use of Discourse Analysis in the Study of Children's Perceptions of South Africa*. Conference paper, Dept of Psychology, University of Cape Town.

Rose, R. and McAllister, I. (1990) *The Loyalties of Voters: A Lifetime Learning Model*. London: Sage.

Rossiter, J. and Palmer, R. (1990) *Northern NGOs in Southern Africa: Some Heretical Thoughts*. Paper presented to the University of Edinburgh, Centre of African Studies, Conference on critical choices for the NGO community.

Rumboldt, M. *et al*. (1994) 'The impact of war upon the pupil's growth in Southern Croatia'. *Child Care, Health and Development*, **20**(3), 189–96.

Scarman, L. (1986) *The Scarman Report*. London: Penguin.

Scase, A. (1989) *Industrial Societies*. London: Unwin.

SCF (undated) *Children in Difficult Circumstances*. London.

SCF (1992) *Country Report, South Africa*. London.

SCF (1993) *Country Report, Mozambique*. London.

Schwartz, R.E. (1982) 'Children under fire: the role of the schools'. *American Journal of Orthopsychiatry*, **53**(3), 409–19.

Schwarzwald, J. *et al*. (1993) 'Stress reaction of school-age children to the bombardment by SCUD missiles'. *Journal of Abnormal Psychology*, **102**(3), 404–10.

Shor, I. (1986) *Culture Wars*. London: Routledge and Kegan Paul.

Silove, D.M. (1988) 'Children of apartheid: a generation at risk'. *The Medical Journal of Australia*, **148**, 346–53.

Skrimshire, A. (1981) 'Community schools and the education of the social individual'. *Oxford Review of Education,* **7**(1).

Smit, J. (1952) 'A study of the critical requirements for instructors of general psychology courses'. *University of Pittsburg Bulletin*, **48**.

Smith, A. (1993) *Labour Party Local Government Conference*. Bournemouth.

Snape. J. (1992) 'Stress in lecturers: a proposed theoretical model for the further education arena'. *Education Today*, **42**(4), 26–31.

Snook, I. A. (ed.) (1972) *Concepts of Education*. London: Routledge and Kegan Paul.

Sterns, S. (1993) 'Psychological distress and relief work: Who helps the helpers?' *Refugee Participation Network,* **15**, 328.

Stuvland, R. (1993) *School Age Children Affected by War: The UNICEF Program in Former Yugoslavia*. New York: UNICEF.

The Student's Charter (1993) London: HMSO.

Thurow, L. (1992) *Head to Head*. New York: Morrow.

Ulrich, P. and Theilman, V. (1993) 'Ethics and economic success'. *Journal of Business Ethics*, **12**(11), 897–98.

UNICEF (1987) *Children on the Front-line*. New York.

UNICEF (1989) *The Situation of Children and Women in Mozambique*. New York.

UNICEF (1990a) *Children in Especially Difficult Circumstances*. New York.

UNICEF (1990b) *The Psycho Social Impact of Violence on Children in Central America*. New York.

UNICEF (1992) *Rehabilitation of Children in Armed Conflict*. New York.

UNICEF (1993a) *Helping Children Cope with the Stresses of War. A Manual for Trainers of Trainers*. New York.

UNICEF (1993b) *Childhood Trauma: Understanding and Treatment*. New York.

Veale, A. (1993) *Training Street Educators and Youth Workers*. Refugee Programme Centre, Oxford (unpublished).

Victor, P. (1972) *The economics of pollution*. London: Macmillan.

Volunteer Centre Berkhamsted (1990) *Voluntary Activity*. Berkhamsted.

Waldron, J. (1988) 'Locke, toleration and the rationality of persecution'. In Mendus, S. *Toleration and the Limits of Liberalism*. London: Macmillan.

Warnock, M. (1979) *Schools of Thought*. London: Faber.

Wedell, D.H., Parducci, A. and Roman, D. (1989) 'Student perceptions of fair grading: a range-frequency analysis'. *American Journal of Psychology*, **102**(2), 233–48.

Weinbach, R.W. (1988) 'Manipulations of student evaluations: no laughing matter'. *Journal of Social Work Education*, **1** (Winter), 27–34.

Welch, M. (1988) *Holding Time*. London: Century Hutchinson.

Wetchler, J. and Vaughan, K.A. (1991) 'Perceptions of primary supervisor interpersonal skills: a critical incident analysis'. *Contemporary Family Therapy*, **13**(1), 61 9.

White, P. (1983) *Beyond Domination*. London: Routledge and Kegan Paul.

Wilkinson, P. (1986) *Terrorism and the Liberal State*. London: Macmillan.

Williams, B. (1979) *Report of the Committee on Obscenity and Film Censorship* (The Williams Report). London: HMSO.

Williamson, J. and Moser, A. (1987) *Unaccompanied Children in Emergencies*. Geneva: International Social Service.

Williamson, J. (1988) *Guidelines for Interviewing Unaccompanied Minors and Preparing Social Histories*. New York: UNCHR.

Willis, P. (1981) *Learning to Labour*. Aldershot: Gower Press.

Wing, L. (1988) 'The continuum of autistic characteristics'. In Schopler, E. and Mesibov, G.B. (eds) *Diagnosis and Assessment in Autism*. New York: Plenum.

Wintour, P. (1993) 'Smith sees Labour as the party of ambition'. *Guardian*, 22 March.

Woods, P. (1979) *The Divided School*. London: Routledge and Kegan Paul.

World Bank (1992) *Annual Report*. New York.

World Conference on Education for All (1990) *Meeting Basic Learning Needs: Vision for the*

1990s. Background document. Jomtien.

World University Service (1990) *Refugee Education Policy for the 1990s: Towards Implementing the Refugee Education Charter*. London: Education and Training Working Group.

Wragg, E.C. (1989) Primary Teachers and the National Curriculum. *Research Papers in Education*, 4:3, 17–47.

Wrong D. (1979) *Power, Its Forms, Bases and Uses*. Oxford: Basil Blackwell.

Name Index

Aarons, M. 38, 40, 53
Abu Nasr, J. 69
Acherson, N. 19
Ackerman, B.A. 113
Ager, L. 62
Allen, G. 16, 36, 73, 95
Andrews, C. 37
Arbuthnot, F. 59
Aronowitz, S. 96

Baker, K. 25–6
Ball, S. 4
Baron, S. 4
Barrow, G. 69
Bastiani, J. 37
Baumol, W. 86, 103, 105–6
Bell, D. 102–4
Blaug, M. 12
Bogdanor, V. 99–100
Bonnerjea, L. 67
Boothby, N. 60, 66–7
Bowles, S. 103
Brennan, T. 19
Broadfoot, P. 13
Brown, R.D. 82–4
Brown, W. 48, 54
Brummer, A. 98

Calvo, L. 61, 67
Chanan, G. 8
Charles, Prince of Wales 24
Charnley, H. 67
Chimienti, G. 69
Christie, P. 38–9, 52
Clinton, B. 98, 101
Coase, R. 102
Connelly, M. 44
Crick, B. 26–30
Cummings, C.E. 12

Dahrendorf, R. 21
Danieli, Y. 59, 65–6, 68
Daniels, H. 43
Davis, A.S. 81–2
Dawes, A. 63, 65–6
de Beer, M. 70
Dearing, R. 46
Desjarlais, R. 63, 71, 73
Dewey, J. 4, 20, 27, 71, 107
Dolan, C. 70
Drucker, P. 103–4
du Toit, A. 58, 71–2
Dunnette, M.D. 91
Dworkin, A. 115
Dworkin, R. 115

Edwards, R. 103
Elbedour, S. 61

Feldman, K.A. 84
Fields, R. 73
Fisher, S. 83
Flanagan, J.C. 92
Fozzard, S. 69
Frith, U. 40, 50

Galbraith, J.K. 102
Gamble, A. 97
Garbarino, J. 63–4
Gilchrist, L. 8
Giroux, H. 96
Gittens, T. 38, 40, 53
Gmelch, W.H. 81, 83
Goldenberg, D. 81–2
Goldfarb, R.R. 87
Goodrow-Wicher, C. 25
Grandin, T. 42, 51
Green, A. 4

Subject Index